GEORGINA HARDING

Georgina Harding was born in 1955. Before starting to write full-time, she worked in publishing in London and also in Tokyo. It was her stay in Japan that set her travelling, taking long journeys through India and Southeast Asia, and eventually returning overland to England via China and the Trans-Siberian railway. She now lives in Islington.

She is currently working on her second book, about the Coromandel Coast of Southern India.

sceptre

'It is a tribute to Harding's writing that the rapid change of events has not made her book less relevant . . . Harding's approach is very appealing: slow to reveal herself, quick to form lyrical impressions of landscape and people. Perhaps the sedate, civilised manner of her transport is the key to her engaging style'

Roger Clarke in The Sunday Times

'She was an observant witness travelling through a world on the edge of transformation . . . Georgina Harding's book records glimpses into the lost world of a Balkan tyrant, but also into a more ancient peasant world that may soon now disappear'

Mark Almond in The Times Literary Supplement

Georgina Harding

IN ANOTHER EUROPE
A Journey to Romania

British Library C.I.P.

Harding, Georgina, *1955–*
    In another Europe: a journey to Romania.
    1. Eastern Europe. Description and travel
    I. Title
    914.7

ISBN 0-340-54421-X

Printed and bound in Great Britain for Hodder and Stoughton Paperbacks, a division of Hodder and Stoughton Ltd., Mill Road, Dunton Green, Sevenoaks, Kent TN13 2YA. (Editorial Office: 47 Bedford Square, London WC1B 3DP) by Clays Ltd., St Ives plc.

For David

The revolving globe of the earth has become very small, and, geographically speaking, there are no longer any uncoloured areas on it. In Western Europe, however, it is enough to have come from the largely untravelled territories in the East or North to be regarded as a visitor from Septentrion, about which only one thing is known: it is cold.

Czeslaw Milosz, *Native Realm*

Foreword

The first edition of this book was published in February 1990. When it went to the printers a few months earlier, it reflected a world still current: yet in December 1989, in less time than it would take for the printed pages to be bound, a riot in Timişoara ignited a revolution, the Romanian régime was overthrown, Nicolae Ceauşescu and his wife were summarily executed – and my book, which had been conceived in part as a protest, became history.

When I travelled to Romania in the autumn of 1988 the country seemed caught in time. A picture of the few weeks I spent there might almost stand for as many decades. Development was held suspended, in the countryside where haymakers worked to a pre-industrial rhythm, and in the Orwellian towns where the second world war might only just have ended. (Perhaps, now, Romanians will look back on the forty years of the Communist era as a single frozen frame in their country's history, as the reel starts again – however erratically – to roll.)

Was there action out of shot? As a passing traveller I could see only the surface – and the surface was about all that any Romanian would dare to reveal. I could perhaps sense something of what lay beneath, but if I perceived a tension in the air, even if I got so far as to feel that I was travelling in the lull before a storm, I could not have imagined that the storm would take the form it did. In October 1988, even in October 1989, most observers in Romania and outside considered Ceauşescu to be unassailable: the black cloud on the horizon was that of the system-isation of the villages, threatening the people of the country and not their ruler. Only now with hindsight does it seem logical that events occurred as they did, that Ceauşescu's power was as brittle as it was hard, and that the pent anger of the people must finally, at some indeterminate moment, express itself as forcefully as it was repressed in the past.

Since the revolution I have had news from a few of those I met in Romania – all disguised in the book, as seemed necessary at the time of writing. 'Nicolae' sent a post card from Vienna, where he was reunited with his family, and the 'Melzers' had left at last for Germany. I wish them all luck.

Georgina Harding
London, December 1990

IN
ANOTHER
EUROPE

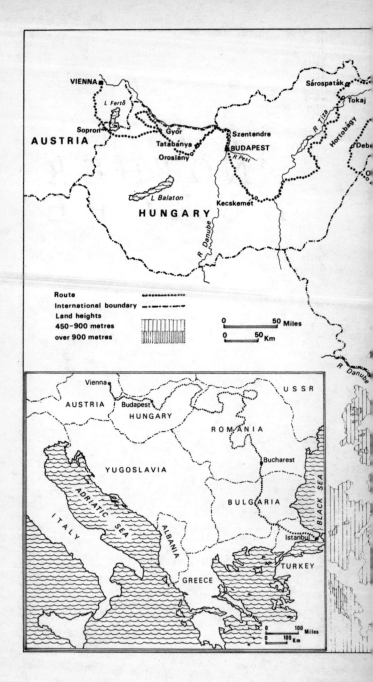

1

The Danube hides away in the plain where it enters Hungary, breaking into streams that meander among willow-covered islands. One broad stream called the Moson Danube snakes off to form the long island of Szigetköz; it rejoins the Danube proper sixty kilometres or so to the south-east. This river too is unobtrusive in its course. You come upon it quite suddenly, seeing a green shimmer between the trees on its bank or a watery light reflected on their leaves. But soon it winds off again from the road. Riding further on you begin to recognise the signs: a bar of trees across the fields that is slightly more solid than others, a strip of tall poplars fringed with eucalyptus, willow or acacia. In the sunlight the acacias stand out like yellow plumage against the papery grey of the poplars.

The road cuts straight, for the most part, through fields of stubble. The young walnuts on each verge cast only small, sharp shadows. Enough for a brief rest, stretched on the dark circle of grass, cycle leant against the whitewashed tree trunk, until the sun moves the shade away. The water in the drinking flask is lukewarm: August is hot in the centre of Europe.

Village boys pass on rattling bicycles, two up, and bump along a track that crosses a field and rises on to what must be the river embankment. I follow them to the beach. Others are already there, swimming, tickling fish, or swinging above the river on a Tarzan creeper, to let go and fall in a thin bronzed streak. The river is sluggish; the greeny-brown water seems almost glaucous, trailing viridian patches of weed. A shower of white seeds is blown on to the surface; they twirl and drift, revealing the patterns of the current over mud banks and shallows. On a wooden landing stage some child's grandmother writes a postcard on the back of a paperback book: *The Adventures of Robin Hood*, in Hungarian. Water glints like mercury through the cracks between the warped planks.

A fat man leans his bike against a tree close to mine and nods to me, rolling up his sweatshirt to air his paunch. Where have I come from, he asks in German, Vienna? Going to Budapest?

'Yes.'

'You must have strong legs.'

I was going further but did not say.

I seemed to have lost direction on Hungary's straight roads, drifting in the sun as on a childhood cycle ride. Forgotten Oxfordshire lanes, blinkered by tall hedges, came to mind like some recurrent tune, in particular a place where gipsies camped, a wide verge sheltered by elms. (I don't think we ever saw the gipsies, my brother and I, as we raced past – he always ahead, I chasing behind – only their dogs, and drab washing strung on lines between the caravans.)

2

When I was a child Europe ended in a jagged north-south line the other side of Germany – West Germany, though one didn't bother to call it that – and Austria. Rather than coming to a distinct end, it petered out into a vague Not-Europe like an early cartographer's unknown region, to meet somewhere with Asia. At school in the 1960s I got the impression that the lands out there were uniformly grey, though the more westerly ones might be a shade paler than Russia itself. Very occasionally a spark of colour brightened the void: the music of Chopin or Liszt, an image of horsemen, or of a town of Gothic towers that might have been torn from an illuminated manuscript. That colour was always historical; images closer to the present came in grainy black and white: Auschwitz, the Warsaw Ghetto, Hungary '56 and Prague '68.

Gradually the void took on the fascination of mystery. There were the photographs of André Kertész. Hungary in the 1910s and '20s: Jewish street accordionists and wandering violinists, a peasant boy sprawled on the grass before a long horizon of poplars. Most of the Jews had gone now, but who remained?

As for the politics, I was simply curious. So much had been said, so little actually seen. I was curious most of all to feel how deep the influence of politics reached: was life really different over there? The propaganda of the Cold War had always said it was. The restrictions had been well publicised but one could not tell how real they were, nor what they would mean day to day. Might there not be something else besides? Much of the writing Eastern Europeans published in the West – inevitably, the writing of dissent – had a vigour of a kind too often absent in our own; it suggested that, in opposition, they had preserved some sense of value we had lost in our fat democracies.

The first sight I had of Eastern Europe, I was coming from Asia. Returning to England on the cheap, I spent £120 on a train ticket from

Peking to Berlin. I had been in the Far East for two years. And from the first stop in Russia, out on the Mongolian border in a railway station of painted wooden houses where log stoves burned, I had a sense of homecoming. West of the Urals, where the late November snow was still thin and underlaid with green, where the forests were broken with fields and the sky was an English grey, I began to feel I belonged; beyond Moscow, as the train crossed Byelorussia, Poland and East Germany, I looked out of the smeared window and wondered how I could be so ignorant about places that looked so familiar. Wintry figures stood beside bicycles at level-crossings waiting for the train to pass, were swiftly overtaken as they pedalled down a straight road parallel to the line. They lived in foursquare houses in a horizontal landscape that could have been a stretch of East Anglia. It was then that I thought of taking my own bicycle and joining them.

That was a couple of weeks after Brezhnev's death in 1982. Six years later when my idea took shape – matured now into a journey from Vienna to Istanbul – the grey East seemed to have begun a process of transformation inspired by Gorbachev. Even the Western press had begun to allow it a little colour.

I took a train to Vienna. I spent just a day in the city, all the morning at a bicycle shop getting a new wheel to replace one buckled in transit. The new wheel was expensive: handbuilt, double-rimmed, whatever that meant – strong, anyway, for the potholed roads the mechanic said I would be sure to encounter. He was arrogantly fit, with tanned legs and ballooning calf muscles beneath harlequin cycling shorts. He said the shop was on a good site just a couple of blocks from the station. Customers were regularly directed there from the registered luggage counter and they always got the best of service: so long as the forms were filled in correctly, Austrian Railways would not fail to pay up.

The afternoon was sultry. In the park alongside the Ringstrasse, which circled the monumental centre, fat women and flabby young men in shorts were walking miniature dogs. Half the pavement by the Ring was designated a cycle lane. Few pedestrians stepped on to it though traffic was decorous: one passing cyclist, a fragile youth with narrow face and wire-rimmed spectacles, politely reminded me to keep to the right. The streets had a smalltown quiet, as if the majority of the Viennese had retreated into shuttered apartments to sleep off a heavy lunch. No music came from the dance schools which were advertised at courtyard entrances with gilded letters on black glass plates. I was impatient to be gone. The city seemed starchy and middle-aged. Even the Danube was corsetted between concrete banks.

Hungary was a little more than a day's ride away. I left next morning. The sky was hot and wide over a plain that was sliced into long strips of stubble, sunflowers and maize. Europe extended monotonously eastwards from one yellow village church to the next.

The border was on the crest of a slight hill, letting me freewheel down into Sopron. A tower-block development stood, according to stereotype, on the edge of the little town, but around a corner the dreary view evaporated amid baroque towers and Gothic spires. Houses and churches were crowded together within the oval of the old fortifications: flaking peachy stucco, steep red roofs and bulbous green belfries. In old wooden shop fronts stood dusty pyramids of tins; in the hosier's, nylon stockings stretched like ribbons around a maypole. Few cars were parked on the cobbled roads in front, and those there were seemed appropriate to period, like the cars on 1950s postcards.

There was a café on the square at the centre of the old town. It was Saturday and Saturday was the day for weddings. Every twenty minutes or so a newly married couple came down the double staircase of the town hall and paused for photographs and congratulations outside its pompous galleried front. The couples looked young, barely twenty: most of the grooms were dark, with fine, narrow faces and preened moustaches, in cream-coloured suits with a red carnation in the button-hole; the brides were more often blonde (I suspected this could not be genes), sharp-featured, swathed in lace. To Western eyes, the scene was nostalgic, however self-consciously modern the tight lurex glitter of the dresses worn by female relations. Was it two, or three, decades behind? The car awaiting each party on the cobbles was the standard Lada, adorned with a spray of red or white gladioli. Couple after couple drove off with a blare of pop music from rolled-down windows.

On Sunday the same cars or others like them flocked out from the town to the beach on the nearby lake, windsurfers strapped to the roofs. The lake, called Fertő in Hungarian, Neusiedlersee in German, straddles the Austrian border. There was an army post on the causeway that ran up to it through the surrounding marsh, manned by boy soldiers to whom papers seemed the vaguest of formalities; I had left passport and permit at the hotel but was waved on with a grin. The waiting cars were held up less by the official barrier than by the herd of caramel-coloured cows which came down the track and flowed around them.

The lake is shallow, probably wadeable in parts, and the spit that divides off the swimming lagoon is surmounted by a line of tall wooden watchtowers. These seemed already a relic of the Iron Curtain, irrelevant to the teenagers on the beach, the long tanned boys playing football or the girls in fluorescent bikini briefs who held to their ears radios tuned to Austrian pop stations.

A family from the eastern city of Miskolc claimed the patch of grass next to mine, a man with a dark moustache and his golden wife, who carried their small daughter spreadeagled across her waist. Both spoke a little English. They were touring western Transdanubia on holiday. Though Hungarians could since the beginning of the year acquire passports freely, foreign exchange rules, and the rates themselves, still made it hard to travel abroad. Our talk soon gave way to the stupor of the sunshine, but not before I got a solution to a puzzle: traffic regulations specifically prohibited cycling on major roads classified with a single digit, yet according to the maps it was impossible to enter certain towns without using those roads; how did bicycles get there?

'That is a stupid law,' the man said. 'Pay no attention.'

'What if the police stop me?'

'If they do, remember that they are fools. Not gentlemen like your English police. You may say yes to everything but pay no attention.' He flicked his hand as if to drive away a fly.

A week later, in a restaurant in Budapest, I met two Sheffield policemen on holiday. 'Do you get stopped a lot?' one asked as soon as he heard how I was travelling. I admitted that I hadn't been stopped at all and repeated what the man had said. They were taken aback: could law enforcement be so lax anywhere in the Soviet bloc?

I passed Lake Fertő again when I left Sopron. Early in the morning it shimmered like a mirage between fingers of marsh. Close to the eastern tip of the lake was the great Esterházy palace at Fertőd, once known as Esterháza. In the eighteenth century it was a middle-European Versailles, painted ochre and white, frivolous and rococo. Haydn lived for twenty years in the Music House. But in the staid nineteenth century the Esterházys deserted Fertőd for Eisenstadt and Vienna. It started to decay then, was badly damaged late in the second world war, and has since been restored piecemeal. Though the palace was closed that day I could walk up to it, cup my hands against the window glass and look through to salons, one opening on to another, right through the house to the fountain in the inner courtyard. The gardens had been modelled on those of Le Nôtre. Dark cones of topiary cast triangles of shade on to the rough dry lawns.

Apart from the palace there was little to stop for: roads lined with fruit trees, kilometre stones neatly posted. I saw that many of the road signs were pitted and rust-marked as if they had been peppered with shot – was this evidence of a familiar flatland boredom? (In the Lincolnshire fens is a hamlet called Twenty; it perhaps had twenty houses once or it may be twenty miles from somewhere. Beneath the village sign stands another sign, 'Twinned with the Moon', and on that someone once sprayed the grafitti 'No atmosphere.') The kilometre stones emphasised the distances. I tried to ignore them. But I found myself automatically counting almost every one, then doing arithmetic in my head, converting into miles the distance to the next town: divide by eight, multiply by five; then working the sum backwards to check the result before the next stone was reached and I could begin again.

Győr was a big industrial town but it had a fine Austro-Hungarian centre that was bright with ochre paint as if the scaffolding had come down only that morning. The hotel was new, converted from a baroque monastery. The young man at the reception desk might have come straight off the peg. He was crisp and handsome, his English precise – as no doubt were his German and his French, acquired at the state's best catering college. With a courtesy that would have suited the Ritz, he carried my bicycle down to the basement where it would be safe for the night. I feared lest a drop of chain oil smear his pressed trousers.

'Where do you go from here?'

'To Budapest, then Romania, Bulgaria, and on to Istanbul.'

'Ah. You must be a student. Many Western students travel.' He spoke without curiosity. 'But I do not think you will enjoy Romania. In Romania, you know, there is nothing.'

I ate at a restaurant on a freshly restored square. The Hungarians who shared the long table told me that it was new too. It had opened only a couple of nights earlier and was probably privately run; you could usually tell when the state had a hand in things.

Was everything in the town new?

One woman in the group spoke fluent English; she worked as a translator at the local Raab truck factory. 'This is how they do things here, always in big projects. Big projects look best on paper. For years the whole town was crumbling. Then the workers came. Then, after a few more years, it is all finished at once. You know, I was born in Győr. My parents' apartment is close by. Only yesterday they were saying to me and to my sister how wonderful it is now. Every building here means something to them. They remember the war and how it was after.'

Éva was vibrant, a little plump, with a shock of hennaed hair; a single barbaric earring danced against her neck as she talked. She said her parents were proud of Győr today and of the opportunities their children had now. But really there was little going on; it was impossible to get a place of your own, almost as difficult to get a job in Budapest. 'Soon it will not matter for me. I am going to West Germany to get married, to a man I met when I went to study there. In Germany we can get a house and good jobs.' She said housing was so short in Hungary that couples had to live with one or the other's parents for years while every weekend they went to a little plot on the edge of the town and built houses for themselves brick by brick. If it weren't for that she would have persuaded her fiancé to come to Hungary. 'He likes Budapest. Even he admits that the Germans do not know how to enjoy life like the Hungarians.'

'Will you find other Hungarians in Germany?'

'Oh yes. For sure. It is impossible to go far in any direction without meeting a Hungarian. For such a small nation we have covered a lot of the world. There is an old joke. Question: what is the world language? You might think English, French, Spanish. But no, the answer is Hungarian because there is a Hungarian everywhere.'

'But it's an impossible language.' (Hungarian has nothing in common with any other European language apart, very distantly, from Finnish. I despaired of picking up anything except by serious study.)

'That is your loss. Believe me, Hungarian is one of the world's great literatures. But how many Hungarian writers have you read? It is never translated. We poor Hungarians must learn all your languages instead!'

I asked what was the first foreign language taught in schools: Russian?

'Yes. But we are not interested in Russian. The teachers want to teach it no more than the pupils want to learn it. And the text books are antiquated: they would not tell you how to buy a train ticket.

Besides, Russian sounds ugly to us. We Hungarians have a musical ear.'

'But the Russians have some great writers.'

'Oh, Tolstoy, Dostoyevsky, Gogol, Chekhov. They read much better in the Hungarian language; nobody would bother to read them in Russian. Personally I prefer the French.'

Ferenc, who sat opposite, had been listening all along. He seemed to understand but would not venture into English before the rest. Now he interrupted and Éva had to translate. 'He says that intellectuals in the West let the Russians pull the wool over their eyes. He says that he trained in film-making and had to study every one of Eisenstein's films. He asks, why do Western Europeans make such a cult of Eisenstein? In Hungary we think his work is crude, just a lot of clumsy expressionism and oblique camera angles.'

Éva and Ferenc walked back with me to the hotel down streets that were shiny with moisture after a momentary shower. I told them that I planned to go to Istanbul. They laughed at my travelling by bike; didn't I know that here a bicycle was peasant transport? But when I said I was going through Romania they turned solemn.

'Do not go to Romania,' Éva said. 'There is nothing there.' That was just what the receptionist had said.

'There's the Carpathians. Transylvania.'

'But you know there is no food? No petrol?'

'That at least I don't need.'

'No light bulbs to see by . . .'

Ferenc put a soft hand on my shoulder and spoke now in surprisingly good English. 'Can I tell you a story?

'I have a friend who was in Transylvania some weeks ago. There are many Hungarian people who live in Transylvania, you understand? My friend is driving through a Hungarian village. And a little girl, five, six years old, comes out in the road. She sees his car, his Hungarian number, and looks to left and right, up and down. There is no-one. Then she waves, but a little wave, like this, so that if someone is behind they cannot see.' He mimed a timid wave, fluttering a hand in front of his stomach, fingers splayed. 'People are frightened there, and this year more than ever.'

*   *

Éva was driving to Budapest the next day and offered me a lift. 'You will find the countryside very boring.'

Only a couple of months later, when I reached Turkey, did I feel no honour was lost in throwing the bike on to the back of a truck and accepting a ride in the cab. I refused her offer, and then regretted it. A week away from home I still found my solitude strange. Echoes of Éva's talk slowly distorted and faded as I cycled on under a blank sky. There were the beginnings of hills ahead to the south-east, beyond the great fields of stubble and of maize that was turning purply-brown at the tips. The fields looked well farmed, the villages tolerably well kept. I knew the shape of the villages by now. They ribboned behind Meccano telegraph poles and verges that were sometimes bedded with flowers. At the centre would be the paired churches, Catholic and Protestant and both closed, the bar and the ABC supermarket, each with bicycles against the rails outside, and the ice-cream stall with a cluster of leathery-faced old women before it. The houses, mostly single-storey, presented only a stuccoed side wall to the road and faced on to a long rectangular yard. A few were still of peasant thatch and whitewash, with vegetable patch, well and wooden granary in the yard, and chickens or geese and white ducks or ugly red-billed Muscovies. Newer houses of concrete and breeze blocks had proud gardens of dahlias and gladioli behind clipped bushes and high metal fences.

At each village in turn I thought of stopping: to buy an ice-cream, steal an apple from a tree on the verge, cool down with water from one of the pumps that were sited at regular intervals along the road. But I would pass through before I could make the decision, on to the next place, held by the silent rhythm of the journey.

Then came coal-mining country. The change was marked by a hillside chopped into allotments, each patch with a triangular-roofed hut like a toytown development. A rusted pulley carried coal from the mine to a plant on the edge of the town of Oroslány, creaking overhead as the bike bounced over a road rutted by heavy machinery, past a home-bound shift of black-faced miners. The town streets were squeezed between the high grey cliffs of apartment blocks. I did stop now, but self-consciously, feeling myself to be an alien observer of things too ordinary to be observed: women in aprons on a balcony, a man in a doorway with a bucket of gladioli for sale, a bucolic frieze on the side of an urban building. Before I left I took a photograph of the monument outside the railway station; it depicted a trio of rough-cast

Stakhanovites with pick-axes raised above their heads. A group of schoolgirls burst into giggles as they passed.

The mining centre of Tatabánya was only fifteen kilometres further on but I did not reach it that night. I turned off the road to see a ruined hermitage in the forest between the two towns and was caught in a storm.

The storm came up behind me as I entered the wood. First, a wind that sent leaves swirling and bent young trees backwards, then a yellow sand cloud that reared up and took away the sky and coated every surface with grit. A long moment later came a rush of hail and then thunder and torrential rain. I could hear branches tearing in the trees. At the hermitage gate I met the caretaker, who took me by the arm and pulled me towards her house, even as I hung back to gape at the speed of the storm and its eerie light. No-one who knew such weather wasted a second out of doors.

Two other women were already sheltering in the house. They drew up a third chair to the oak table where they sat in the hall, beneath a heavy carved crucifix. They were Slovaks, mother and daughter. The mother spoke some Hungarian; the southern district she came from had been a part of Hungary until 1920. The daughter spoke English so that between us all we managed an indirect communication. The Slovaks were travelling by bus and on foot, visiting abbeys and religious sites; they might have been pilgrims for all the luggage they carried, rolled up in a single home-made sausage bag of chequered cotton and now hung to dry in the kitchen.

The caretaker was a tiny, dark, intense woman. She and her husband lived reclusively in the woods. Bookshelves stretched along every whitewashed wall of the house; his, on theology and engineering, hers, unclassifiable: literature from Tolstoy to Maugham to Updike, biographies of artists and opera singers, guides to countries from Japan to Peru.

'Do you paint?' I asked.

'No, only read.'

'Have you travelled much?'

'No,' she said, 'never outside Hungary.'

Her husband was little taller than she, a darting man of chameleon moods. 'How do you do, you may call me Emil-Miklós,' he introduced himself with assumed British formality – and almost every word of

English that he knew. But then he skipped up the hall to his desk and his short-wave radio to gather reports on the storm. While it thundered outside he twiddled the dials frenetically, filling the narrow room with a restless radio crackle. When the storm died, he stopped, turned solemn and monkish, announced that now he would show us around.

It was just before sunset when we went out. The clouds had reefed back, baring a turquoise sky. Light gleamed on the white hermitage walls and the wet grass. A skinny child who lived in one of the other houses came to show off a giant snail he had found. Even as he held it in his hand the snail stretched out its body to bask in the sudden moisture. This was the first real rain Hungary had had in more than two months.

The dozen or so plain houses were set in a rectangle within the enclosure, at their centre the tower of the ruined eighteenth-century church. A group of strange-looking bells hung from horizontal poles on the lawn before the tower. Emil-Miklós demonstrated them to us. Each one produced a different note according not only to its size but to the positioning of the narrow openings in its sides. He announced mysteriously that the inventors of the bells, in Budapest, were working on the casting of a giant bell which would be the largest in the world and would be a symbol of peace. Why peace? I asked. Because these bells were made of aluminium, he answered, not of gunmetal like ordinary bells. In the past, too many of the bells of Central Europe had been taken down from village belfries and recast into guns.

He shook off his solemn air as swiftly as he had adopted it, and took us inside the hermitage houses. These had been restored, or rather rebuilt, as élite holiday homes, each allocated to a factory or government department. Like an agent for a villa timeshare, he pointed out the tiled bathroom in each one, the new cooker in the kitchen and the central heating system, prodded each bed and switched on the television to prove it was colour.

We slept in the one house that was unfinished, warned that we must be out the next day before the decorators arrived. Emil-Miklós found for us one foam mattress. I offered it to the older Slovak woman, who looked grey and frail, but she would use it no more than she would take the food the Hungarians had offered. They had no such soft beds at home, she said. It was I must have the mattress. I would be cold on the stone floor. Early next morning I walked down to the road with them under a gentle and constant rain. They had repacked their things in the sausage bag without a glance at my well-equipped panniers and impenetrable waterproofs. It was an absurd battle to persuade them to take the one useful thing I had to spare: a large plastic bag which would keep their luggage dry. I saw them on to the bus before cycling off in the drizzle, head down, across the Vértes hills towards Budapest.

3

'Come for the race?'

A German cyclist panted beside me at a level crossing on the outskirts of Budapest.

'What race?'

One foot to the ground, he rested his bulk a moment. Where he wasn't red from exertion, sunburn took over. His bicycle must have needed all his weight to steady it, the rear wheel was so loaded with bulging panniers and camping gear rolled up in pink cellophane.

'The Grand Prix.'

'You mean a cycle race?'

'No, a motor race.' He yelled as the train went by. 'The Hungarian Grand Prix.'

The road into the city ran flat and straight, parallel to the Danube but always a block or two away so that the river was unseen. Only close to the centre did hills press down from the west and force the traffic out into the sharp light of the embankment. The river brought the smell of mud with it. Long strings of barges slipped downstream beneath the monumental Chain Bridge.

As I crossed the bridge a helicopter roared in over the water, wheeled overhead and dropped to a landing stage beneath the smoked-glass front of the Atrium Hyatt Hotel. The bright crowd among the fluttering umbrellas on the hotel terrace surged forward to see who got out. The helicopter took off again, back the way it had come. In the forecourt of the Forum Hotel, the Atrium Hyatt's equally glassy American twin, more people pressed to see a Formula One car on display, a garish yellow Lotus. I stopped close by. In the crowd the rush of Hungarian was dominated by a fast clamour of Italian. The city had been taken over for the weekend by dark Latins in multicoloured shirts who parked their cars askew on the streets or lolled astride 1000cc motorcycles.

And they had taken all the hotel rooms. 'No reservations, no rooms,' yelled the clerk at the mob in the tourist office, alternately in Italian and English. 'We are sorry, even private lodgings are full up. Stay at the university and come back tomorrow. We open at nine.'

In the Hotel Universitat student Interail travellers mixed with the Grand Prix set; they waited fatalistically, perched among the rucksacks that were spewed across the filthy floors. At the desk I was given a form to fill in. 'When you hand this in we give you a number. Come back in two hours and we will be able to allocate you a room.'

I mistrusted central planning. I spent the two hours wandering around the smaller hotels and eventually spoke to someone who knew someone who could give me lodgings. And found a quiet room in Buda – quiet save for the yellow trams that clattered up and down the steep hill outside – and a landlady who had been an Olympic fencer, Tokyo 1964. (Alone on the living-room wall in the cramped flat hung a framed certificate: the Hungarian women's team won the gold medal that year.)

The Danube is wide here and cuts the city cleanly in two. On the west is Buda, with old houses and terraced gardens climbing steep Castle Hill. This is the historic citadel but its white Gothic bastions are nineteenth-century and the Dominican monastery behind them is only a façade for the Hilton Hotel. It has been almost entirely rebuilt and restored since the war; even the cobbles on the roads are new and smoothly laid. Buda is more alive in the dilapidated streets on the sides of the hill, where the apartment houses are discoloured and pockmarked, with walls propped up by rough wooden buttresses and tilting balconies hung with creepers. In Fő utca, the narrow street which runs along the base of the hill close to the river, the low domes of old Turkish baths squat among baroque churches and random apartment housing from the last three centuries.

Across the river, Pest stretches into the Great Plain. Though its foundations go back earlier than those of Buda, Pest feels like a town with a short life, a late nineteenth-century boom town. Following the Austro-Hungarian Compromise of 1867, when the Habsburgs shared power with the Hungarians, Budapest became the empire's second capital. Parisian ring roads and boulevards, great commercial buildings like those of London and Liverpool, imperial monuments that echoed Vienna, were thrown up in a rush. A neo-classical gallery was built for the national art collection, a neo-Gothic palace for the parliament.

Eiffel & Cie of Paris sent designs for a railway station. And as this was Central Europe there was also a yellow-ochre opera house, a park with a castle folly that might have come from Zenda, and a couple of grand spa hotels.

On the Pest side of the Chain Bridge is the Gresham Building, an art-nouveau memorial to capitalist pomp. A plaque to the left of the entrance records that it was built by the Gresham Life Assurance Society in 1906 and lists the then directors: wing-collared Edwardians with names like Thornthwaite, Beadnell, Butterworth, Courtenay, Fooks and Sir Edward Fitzgerald Law. On the other side are the engraved and gilded names of their Hungarian counterparts. The gates are decorated with sinuous wrought-iron peacocks. Beside them was once the entrance to the Gresham Restaurant. Even after 1918, when the boom was over and the empire dismantled, and Hungary was enclosed within its present tight boundaries, the Gresham was renowned. But now youths mutter to passing tourists at the gate and do black-market deals in the stagnant light of the arcade behind. The art-nouveau arabesques barely show beneath the grime on the tiled walls.

Pest is a decaying city. For every one restored block or new building, modernist or post-modernist, there are streets of crumbling walls you could walk until the soles of your feet hurt. But the people of Pest disregard them like a sloughed skin. They pack the pavements and strut through the traffic on the roads. At courtyard entrances tiers of signs and nameplates advertise the private shops and businesses that mushroom within the block: dressmakers, dentists, chiropractors, hairdressers. The balconies on the courtyards overflow like baroque urns, filled with petunias and begonias, and morning glory trained up wires.

It is the state which owns most of the apartment buildings; leaseholders are not responsible for their upkeep. So chandeliers and oriental carpets may sometimes be glimpsed through open doorways off stairwells that smell of cabbage. More often the high-ceilinged rooms have been partitioned into vertical boxes, where an extended family is crammed into a single flat.

For three months at the end of the second world war, the Russians and Germans fought street by street through Budapest. Pest was liberated in mid-January 1945 but the Germans had blown the bridges and were not driven out of Buda until 13 February. The palace and the public buildings of Castle Hill were almost devastated, and scarcely a house elsewhere was untouched. Forty years later, on both sides of the river, stone and stucco are still pitted with holes made by bullets and shrapnel.

Such, at least, was the official story. Budapest also saw street battles in 1956, when ten thousand or so Hungarians were killed by another invading Soviet army. That outburst of Hungarian defiance was quelled within two weeks. Thirty-two years later what was officially known as a counter-revolution was still taboo.

'Remember, all the bullet holes you see are from the second world war. You won't find any from the uprising: they've been plastered over.' Zoltán Kovács cynically explained Budapest to a foreigner.

He was an old boyfriend of Éva's. I called him up when I arrived and we met late one afternoon in the Café Angelica. The dim café was full at that hour with Buda matrons who brooded and clucked amid mahogany and flowered porcelain.

Zoltán was neat and dark, plump over his small frame like an oriental. His pointed beard was turning to grey. His scarlet shirt and faded blue jeans did just enough to proclaim him an intellectual, as did the battered leather satchel stuffed with proofs he was taking home to work on. He was an editor and translator, and probably very good at his job, if he worked as he spoke. His English was polite, almost too exact, as if his small mouth held back each phrase until it had been checked and punctuated.

We had Viennese coffee and sweet cakes. Zoltán watched the brimming cream sink and melt in his cup, and asked how Hungary struck me as a traveller. His thoughtfulness required as much in return. I told him that it seemed intangible. It did not feel Communist, unlike Czechoslovakia where I had been the year before. Even superficially. There were few red stars to see and there were Western goods in the shops.

'That is what our leader said the other day. Did you know? Károly Grosz visited Washington earlier this summer. He spoke at a press conference – that in itself was a revolutionary action for a Hungarian politician. And in answer to a journalist's question he said, "Hungary is not a Communist state." We do not know what he meant. Now Mr Grosz is introducing something called "Socialist pluralism". But we do not yet know what that means either. You realise that in the East the words Communism and Socialism are used as if they were interchangeable – or rather, Socialism has become a euphemism for the other?

29

Well, now they may perhaps begin to mean different things here as they do where you come from.'

Zoltán was cautious about the political changes in Hungary that were currently being discussed in the Western press. 'You in the West jump too quickly to conclusions. We here are not so naive.

'Let me tell you a Russian joke – well, not a joke perhaps for it will not make you laugh – a parable. Imagine, a runaway train in a silent movie, belching smoke across the Russian steppe. The passengers lean out of the windows. As the train curves around a long bend they suddenly see the lines up ahead: there are no rails there. The line has not yet been completed. They go to Lenin's compartment. "What is to be done, Comrade Lenin? There are no tracks ahead." Lenin says, "Pay the workers higher wages." But Lenin dies; Stalin sits now on his red plush seat; still there are no rails. Stalin says, "It is a conspiracy among the workers. Dig it out. Find the counter-revolutionaries. Let the guns bark." The workers are shot. Stalin dies, Khrushchev comes. He has a clever solution. "We do not need the past," he says. "Take up the rails from behind and lay them again in front of the train." They run around and do it but they cannot get the rails straight. "What shall we do?" Khrushchev is gone but they ask Brezhnev. He tells them, "Pull down the blinds, Comrades. Sit here and listen to the train say We're-getting-along-fine, we're-getting-along-fine." And so it goes on. Finally, Gorbachev strides into the compartment. "Open the blinds," he says. "Yell so that they can hear you in the distant mountains: THERE ARE NO RAILS."'

Zoltán had tiny hands that fluttered as he spoke. They were almost feminine despite the black hair that ran down from the wrists. But when conversation stopped they stilled and settled shyly. He said little that was personal. He must have been in his mid-forties and had never married, though he had lived with Éva for a while.

He wanted to talk about politics yet he kept a sceptical position on the outside. He described the prevailing passivity in the country. He said people waited to see what happened next like an audience before a cinema screen. They knew the genre well. They did not expect much that would surprise them, but there was always the chance of a twist in the plot. Perhaps the change was for real. But there could be no real pluralism without opposition parties and where were these to come from? Hungarians did not have the habit of democracy. On the contrary, they preserved habits that had been formed under Stalinism. They had perfected the art of dissembling, of appearing to be one thing and becoming another; their conversation had many layers to it, one beneath the other.

'Even now?' I asked.

'As I said, these are habits. I think people here can still be divided into those who agree and those who think otherwise – I prefer to call these the thinkers. It is hard to explain since none of it is black and white. When I talk to someone I can be all the while questioning his motives for expressing a certain opinion or saying something in a particular way; and he is automatically doing the same to me. I feel freer talking to you now, to a foreigner who is not trying to make such a judgement.'

He said it was nothing like it had been once. He was a child in Stalin's time but he could remember some things. He remembered when Stalin's death was announced on the radio. His mother stood washing the dishes at the sink before the window, and she stopped her work immediately. She could not be seen to be doing the washing up at such a time. And there was a boy at his school the next day who would not stand silent for a moment of remembrance: the teacher punished him, though he got a present when he went home that afternoon. 'Perhaps you will see in Romania. Perhaps that is how it is there.'

In Hungary now there was no need for such blatant performances. Yet there were still things the agreers must nod to in order to assure themselves a promotion or their children a place at university. And this was so taken for granted now that there was nothing to stop you agreeing. What reason was there to be a hero?

We went for a walk, down Fő utca to Rose Hill. Up a steep staircase on the side of the hill was a terrace overlooking the Danube, at its centre a Moslem tomb. A saintly dervish, Gül Baba, was buried there; he had fallen to the ground and died in Buda's great Matthias church while the Turks gave thanks following their conquest of the city in 1541. (Curiously, I was to come across a second tomb purporting to contain the same dervish a few months later in Istanbul.)

Gül Baba's death was not, evidently, an ill omen for the Turks: they went on to occupy the city for around one hundred and fifty years, most of central Hungary for longer, though they never got further up the Danube than Vienna. They had left few traces behind them save this tomb, the Turkish baths, some words perhaps and Zoltán's own name. I wondered if there was more: give him a round turban and he could have been a pasha in an Ottoman miniature.

The houses on the hill were unmistakably middle-class. Zoltán said it was Budapest's Hampstead. Dollar as well as *forint* millionaires lived there, people who had made their money since the economic liberalisations of the early 1970s.

'You see we have rich people now in Hungary. See the BMWs. And every house is now installing a satellite dish to watch Western European networks. But do not think we have prosperity. Hungary has the biggest foreign debt in Eastern Europe and the economy is close to collapse. Most people work day and night just to keep up their present standard of living. It is normal to have two jobs and some have three: working in an office and also in a restaurant, and perhaps doing something from home as a handyman or a hairdresser. No one in Budapest has time for you now.

'What is most important for today's Hungarians is not political freedom but money. We are like you. We admire your Mrs Thatcher. It is the new faith.'

Most of Rose Hill's houses were pre-war villas with coloured stucco, wooden shutters and wrought-iron balconies. Bourgeois individualism had raised a Transylvanian turret on one house, given a neo-baroque façade or an elaborate wooden porch to another, and fenced a garden round with a Chinese wall and moon gate. The gardens would be white with cherry and plum blossom in spring; now they were garish with dahlias and rudbeckia, marigolds and hibiscus in neat beds beside sunshaded patios. The racket of the crickets, louder than the distant traffic, was a measure of the suburbanness of the district.

I spent a week in Budapest. One morning I bought an English newspaper in the Atrium Hyatt and read it in the air-conditioned coffee bar.

The Independent. 3 August 1988. A small item: 'Caught in the whirlpool of *glasnost*, Hungary will soon publish its first sex magazine, with Samantha Fox as the cover girl in its first issue.'

A doorman in burgundy uniform and white gloves set the door revolving for me when I went out.

On the metro a man watched his bland reflection in a dark window. He clutched on his lap a shoulder bag made of thick turquoise plastic; Samantha Fox was pictured on it, her name printed underneath. On the bus going to the Bulgarian Embassy I looked over a woman's shoulder and read the headline in her magazine. I guessed at the

Hungarian: Anthony Delon: like father, like son. Alain and Anthony gazed with too-blue eyes from the cheaply printed pages; inset were smaller pictures of one-time girlfriends.

Temperatures had been in the nineties all week. The city seethed like Calcutta. Its vitality and its decay seemed organic, catalysed by the heat and the exhaust fumes. Shoppers on the pavements wore fashionable clothes with square-shouldered pride, girls baring tanned skin from the slightest of mini skirts and sun dresses. Their style shouted their acquaintance with Austrian television advertisements. The only queues I saw in downtown Pest were outside the shops of Benetton and Adidas.

There was a McDonald's in Pest; and around the corner its Hungarian competition, almost indistinguishable, big and probably state-owned. I knew a Hungarian in London, János, who had left illegally in the 1970s. He had told me to look out for the delicious pancakes they sold on the streets in Budapest. He said that the first people to make money out of the economic liberalisations were the pancake-sellers, who had set up stalls with little capital and made huge profits: 'You'll see them everywhere.' But János had been away too long. I found pancake-sellers only in provincial resorts: Budapest had graduated to hamburgers.

Csaba Kis was János's childhood friend; they had grown up on the same street. He was fair, tanned, medium height and medium build. He wore a white linen jacket and appeared on television, a reporter on a popular documentary programme. The most striking thing about him was that he was constantly in motion.

He had told me to meet him outside a big Buda hotel, high-rise and an easy landmark. He barely stopped his car and we drove off over the river. He charged at the traffic: he had a couple of errands to do and a story to draft that evening as well as showing me around; the next day he was going to Miskolc on another story and then he was off to Lake Balaton for the weekend. When we stopped at red lights he pulled a business card from a pocket and scribbled reminders on the back with a two-inch stub of pencil or crossed out jobs already done. We paused in a dim street where a friend of his lived and he wrote a note on another business card and slipped it under the windscreen wiper of his friend's car; he said it was quicker than knocking on the door. Then we went to a bar.

'So how is my friend János? He calls me sometimes but I think he has no money.'

'No, I don't think he has. He says you're to visit him.'

'Maybe I will. What is it now? August. Maybe September I could go to London. Last year I was in California. We have another old friend, János and I, who went to L.A. A film producer now. He has a blue swimming pool like in the pictures of David Hockney.'

His eyes roamed the air as he talked, as if he was a surfer in search of a new wave. 'He's English, David Hockney. János says it's grey in England.'

'It is, a lot of the time.'

'He says it depresses him.'

'It probably depressed Hockney too. Perhaps he went to Los Angeles for the blue skies.'

'Have you been to L.A.?'

'No.'

'When I was there the sky wasn't blue. It was no colour at all.'

'So Hungary's better?'

He laughed. 'It was today. But tell me about János. I worry about him.'

I did not know János very well, enough only to feel that he was disappointed in England. He was a film editor, ever without work.

'When he left he was nineteen. He said Budapest was no place for him. He talked of politics but I think what he wanted was adventure. He had met a Swedish girl, and he had this golden dream of Sweden. You know he went to Sweden first? So he chooses some fantastical method to escape, tied underneath a railroad car or something – I never knew the details. But then he arrives in Sweden and Sweden is boring.'

I thought of him living in a north London tower block. 'And now England's boring too. He wants to go to California.'

'Next month I shall see him. If he has no money I shall take some.'

We were in the bar long enough only for a single quick drink. Csaba raced out again and drove me up Gellért Hill to see the lights of Budapest. He named the bridges over the black gash of the Danube.

'Now I have at least shown you everything, if only from a distance. I must go home and write my piece.' And he kissed my hand; it took a while to get used to the custom.

*   *   *

34

Csaba found the time to have breakfast with me the day I left the city. He looked more golden than before, sitting at a table outside Gerbeaud's coffee house in Vörösmarty Square. Just back from Balaton, he talked of the lake like a Californian of the ocean. Balaton, which is larger than Lac Leman, is Hungary's riviera, surrounded by long beaches, hotels and holiday homes. Csaba had a cabin there. That weekend, he said, the shallow lake was warmer than he could remember, so hot it had been the past few weeks. The water had been wonderful to swim in at night.

He shifted in his chair and tapped his sunglasses on the table top. There seemed to be a single waitress working on the café terrace; we waited almost a half-hour before we could order. Csaba tried to catch the waitress as she passed but she snapped angrily at him.

He was embarrassed. 'I am sorry. You need to be patient here, even at Gerbeaud's. I know things happen faster where you come from.'

'What did she say?' I asked.

'She said, "Life's not all coffee and cakes." But she's a waitress in a coffee house – what else can it be? It's like this everywhere in Budapest nowadays. People are too busy to be polite. And when it's hot like now they get angry. That girl probably does another job at night when this place closes.'

We bought two lottery tickets from an old woman who did the rounds of the tables, a little woman like a bird with a white plume of hair. Csaba charmed her and she stayed and piped away at him for a while. He said that when the lottery was drawn in September we three could share the winnings. As long as I sat there I believed in his luck.

I walked with him as far as the entrance to the Palace of Television. The frothy white building used to be the stock exchange. Now it was one of the few in Budapest that still had a red star on top.

4

The Saturday before I left I had followed the Budapest weekenders out to Szentendre, a few kilometres up the Danube. In a church there I witnessed an extraordinary speech.

Szentendre was a town of yellow baroque streets that climbed steeply from the river bank to the old citadel. There was a festival that August weekend, and the churchyard on the hilltop was filled with trinket and candyfloss stalls. An improvised stage had been set up by the church entrance and the ranks of schoolroom chairs before it had already been disarranged by the dawdling crowd: the first performance of the day, a brass band, was not due to start until two o'clock. Inside the church, a woman was standing by the altar rail addressing a group of people in the front pews. I assumed she was a tour guide and sat down at the back to wait until the talk was finished. It was cool and dim, the frescos of the sanctuary striped with sunlight that came through lancet windows. The building had the gay air of rural baroque; the carved and painted evangelists reared out from the sides of the wooden pulpit like merry-go-round horses.

Only slowly did I realise that this wasn't a tour. There was a compulsive quality in the woman's voice that made me listen, and go on listening though I could not understand the Hungarian. The words seemed to come in crashing waves, mounting and breaking and retracting, rhythmic like those of an ancient storyteller. And with each change of tempo the woman's face changed. It was vivid with feeling. Her skin and hair were dark but her eyes were pale – when I came close to her later I saw that the irises were almost colourless, just ringed grey-blue. Sometimes she dropped her head into shadow but then she would raise it and push back her hair so that a shaft of light fell across her cheek.

I sat there for perhaps a quarter of an hour. When the story at last ebbed away the woman looked emptied, crushed. After a still moment, the men and women in the church began to clap, and many went to her, put their arms around her neck and kissed her. Some of them wept.

This had been more than just a performance. As people began to leave I walked up to the group around the speaker. A grey-haired woman turned to me; she had a schoolteacher's square, practical face. Had I understood it all? she asked. It was about believing. About the church, the past. About Transylvania. She put her arm around the speaker's shoulders. 'About everything. It was like a prophet talking.'

It was alien to me to feel history with such passion. But then I came from England, from villages whose churches show a calm continuity in their Romanesque doors and Gothic vaults, Saxon fonts and eighteenth-century memorials. Too many of Hungary's medieval churches might have been built of sand, levelled in successive raids and invasions: that one on the hilltop in Szentendre was burned down by the Mongols in the thirteenth century, rebuilt, and again destroyed by the Turks three hundred years later. And an Austrian tide had advanced as the Turkish one receded. The Habsburgs may have built new churches but they razed the castles, and ruled the country right up to the twentieth century. Hungary had not even three decades of independence before the Nazis and then the Soviets arrived.

Today, heroes from the nation's various struggles against historic empires are remembered in the street names of every town. Their statues stand in public squares and parks, lined up along the walks like guardians before a Confucian tomb.

Ferenc Rákóczi II was Prince of Transylvania and leader of insurrections against the Habsburgs. His career is played out and replayed in every town museum beneath his ubiquitous portrait: a Magyar aristocrat fit to be one of Dumas' musketeers, with flowing hair and curled moustaches above red lips, velvet cloak with jewelled clasp over one shoulder, the gold medallion of a noble order on a red satin ribbon around his neck. The original painting hangs in his ancestral castle at Sárospatak, along with muskets, daggers and maps; with his tattered banner, decayed to strips of thread pressed between glass sheets; and a red cloak almost wholly worn of its velvet pile. When I went there, a few days after Hungary's Constitution Day, the gallery in the castle sounded with a slow lament from concealed speakers, and three shiny evergreen wreaths ribboned in the national red, white and green had been placed beneath the picture. Rákóczi was still mourned though he died in 1735.

He had died in exile, having spent the last twenty years of his life pestering first the Poles, then the French and the Turks for support in his failed cause. Few Hungarian rebels met with a better end.

Zoltán had given me a simple lesson in his country's history. He took the money from his wallet and laid it out on the polished table at the Café Angelica. 'These are the great Hungarians. Exiles and martyrs. See, on the ten-*forint* note there's our great Sándor Petőfi, member of the 1848 revolutionary committee, killed losing the battle of Segesvár in Transylvania. He was only twenty-six. With the economy as it is here, he'll be discontinued soon. But we still have György Dósza on the twenty-*forint* note. He led the 1514 peasants' revolt and was executed most imaginatively: they burned him alive on a red-hot iron throne. On the fifty-*forint* note, Rákóczi; he died in Turkey. On the hundred-*forint*, Kossuth, our leader of 1848; he died in Italy. On the thousand-*forint*, Béla Bartók, one of the greatest musicians of the century but he died in America. At least he is now buried here: his body was brought over from New York earlier this year.'

'How about the five hundred-*forint*?' It had on it the fine, romantic face of the poet Endre Ady.

'Ady? He was all right. He died of syphilis. In Hungary.' Zoltán grinned. 'Now who do you have on your money in England? Winston Churchill?'

No, but we did have Wellington. And Florence Nightingale.

'Who was she?'

'She was a great nurse, in the Crimean War.'

'Did you win that one?'

I couldn't quite remember. I said I didn't think it had mattered much.

'Of course, you won all the others. It is we small nations who always lose. And even when we come up with a chance, Hungary joins the wrong side. Like in the last war. Why is that?'

Transylvania could be seen as a symbol of Hungary's defeats. The province was part of the medieval Hungarian kingdom but remained autonomous when the rest of the country fell under Ottoman and Habsburg rule, to be reunited with Hungary in 1848. After the first world war, when the Habsburg empire was parcelled out, Transylvania was awarded to Romania. Most of the territory was again held by

Hungary during the second world war but returned to Romania at its close. This is seen by Hungarians as a penalty exacted for the Horthy régime's support for the Nazis. Though in 1940 Romania also had turned to Germany, a timely coup at the very end of the war allowed that country to ally itself with the victors.

Hungarians seem to see Transylvania as the lost mountainous soul of their land. They say that the purest Hungarian qualities were preserved there through the years of foreign domination, that even now the Transylvanian Szeklers – descendants of the Avars or another fellow tribe of the Huns sent in the early Middle Ages to defend the eastern Carpathian frontier – speak the purest form of the Hungarian language. Although the two million or so Hungarians of Transylvania are greatly outnumbered by the Romanians, many Hungarians believe the land is theirs by ancient right. Their historians have argued that the region was practically uninhabited during the age of migrations and was settled gradually from the ninth century onwards by Hungarian tribes; but the Romanians argue that they were there first, that the Romanian peasants are descended from the ancient Dacians who lived there at the time of Trajan's conquest. The weight of the argument appears in truth to fall on the Romanian side; it seems that in the pocket of the Transylvanian Carpathians, alone of all that region, the ancient population was not swept away by the oncoming tribes from the east.

Under the present Romanian government it has appeared that the Hungarian culture in Transylvania is being systematically diluted, though minority rights are in theory assured. It goes like this: Romanian families are settled in Hungarian villages; a Romanian school is set up in addition to the existing Hungarian one – the Romanians are a minority here, minorities must be served; a few years later there are more Romanians, it is illogical to have two schools, they are amalgamated; but more subjects are taught in Romanian than in Hungarian: so the Hungarian language will gradually disappear. A similar pattern occurs in universities and colleges, in local theatres, and in newspapers: in 1973 on the pretext of a paper shortage all newspapers had to reduce size and circulation; later the Romanian-language ones were restored to previous size but the Hungarian ones were not.

Sometimes the assertion of the Romanian claim has reached the absurd. In the town of Cluj, medieval Hungarian gravestones were removed from the cemetery and replaced with Romanian ones. ('What is it that a car thief does first?' asked the Hungarian who told me this: 'Change the number plates.')

In the spring of 1988, when I was planning my journey, news broke of a projected agrarian reform in Romania which would entail the 'systemisation' – effectively, the demolition and resettlement – of seven thousand villages. Details were vague, no-one said quite which villages and when, though the programme was to be completed, in three phases, by the end of the century. But the Hungarians I knew were sure: 'Do you imagine that it is just any village that will be bulldozed? No, it is the Hungarian villages in Transylvania.' They said they could not care less what the Romanians wanted to do in their own country – bulldoze villages and move to high-rise blocks, jump from the balconies or starve – so long as it did not involve the Hungarian minority. And accused the Romanian president of premeditating cultural genocide.

In Budapest on 27 June a previously unthinkable demonstration occurred: Hungarians protested in force against another Warsaw Pact country, Romania. They seemed to have tacit approval from the authorities. Word had been spread by pamphlets distributed in the streets but anyone who had not received a pamphlet could learn from news coverage on Hungarian television and Radio Budapest. Estimates state that between thirty and fifty thousand people gathered in Heroes' Square; many individuals put the figure higher.

In London, János had followed the Transylvanian story avidly, keeping every newspaper cutting. One July evening I stood and talked to him while he mowed the grass in a friend's neglected garden; the grass was long and he raked it into piles with a wooden rake. 'You know, if it were not for Russia, Hungary and Romania would be at war. And if there was a war, I'd go straight back there and fight.'

5

On the Great Plain Hungary seemed a new country like America, wiped clean of the past. A century ago much of it was wild grassland – except where the great slovenly rivers had flooded or where depressions had fostered areas of marsh. Now it is cut into broad rectangles of wheat, maize, sunflowers and paprika. Drainage, irrigation and collective farming have imposed a geometric order broken only by scattered homesteads, low whitewashed houses with haystacks and plum trees in front, loose chickens and tethered cows grazing.

In the fifth century, when the Huns arrived in Europe in the first wave of the barbarian invasions, they chose the Plain as the centre of their empire. Close to the river Tisza near the southern town of Szeged Attila made his capital – if you could call it that, a shanty town of wooden palaces, tents and waggons. The Plain was the last piece of steppe the Huns would encounter west of the Carpathians. It must have seemed a place where a nomad could stop and build a hut without losing his nomadic horizons. Strategically, it was an ideal base from which to launch raids on the rich territories to the south and west: a landscape where horsemen could move fast. To the fearful eyes of the Romans the Huns were as inseparable from their horses as centaurs; the historian Ammianus recorded that they ate, drank, slept, even pissed, on horseback. He said that on foot they could barely walk, bowlegged and stumbling in rough shoes made without lasts. Other tribes swept in behind the Huns: Avars, Slavs, Cumans, Pechenegs and lastly the Magyars, who came from the eastern Urals and the middle Volga and crossed the Carpathians early in the ninth century.

I stayed one night in Kecskemét, a day south from Budapest. In the local museum were finds from nomadic burials. A Magyar horseman was buried with the head of his horse, the horse's skull grotesque and huge beside the crumpled human skeleton.

Though the museum went back to the Bronze Age, to the hunters, cattle-grazers and marsh fishermen who inhabited the Plain before even the Romans came, Kecskemét looked as though it might have been founded in the nineteenth century. It was old-fashioned but not historical, like a hand-coloured postcard: mustard-yellow roads paved in glazed bricks, houses painted ochre, pink, turquoise and mint green, bicycles rested against railings or the peeling trunks of plane trees. Even the sky might have been the work of a studio colourist: too blue above, fading to a pale west over red-tiled roofs.

From there I headed north-east, roughly following the course of the Tisza upstream. Much of the arable land was already under plough and the road was monotonous. For a time I left it to ride along the flood embankment. This was steep, often thick with cow parsley and cornflowers on the side facing the river and with a lush strip of buttercups in the damp ground at its base. From the embankment I could look out across the fields or down through a jungle of gnarled willows to the brown river and the swallows swooping low over the water.

Boys swam at village beaches. I saw one strong swimmer pass boldly downstream in the centre of the river, throwing an even wake right across its breadth as if he was going far. But in practice the tight meanders made it hard to reach a destination and I had to find my way back to the road.

Like America. The villages on the Plain were provincial and dusty, strung along the road. There were few people about in the middle of the day, only grandmothers watching geese or sitting in vine-shaded yards – except for one village where I followed a funeral procession, a dark-clothed, Dodge-City crowd of mourners, up the main street to the cemetery in the fields outside. Elsewhere, what little movement there was centred on the local bar, where bicycles were propped against rails by the door as horses might once have been tied. Inside, past the crates of empties, the men in faded blue overalls who sat beneath girlie calendars paid little attention to strangers.

In the heat I stopped often to drink. Once the girl behind the bar answered my stumbling Hungarian in good English. She was seventeen, just out of school and impatient to be off to university in Budapest that September. Already she was dressed in urban monotone, with straight black skirt and tailored white blouse.

'Why did you come this way? You could have gone through the hills in the north.'

'I just thought that if I came to Hungary, I must come to the Plain. To see what it's like.'

'So what is it like?'

'Flat.'

'You do not have flat country in England?'

'We do. But never a stretch as big as this.'

'How long will it take you to get across?'

'About three days if I don't stop too often.'

'Oh, there is nowhere to stop. I know, I was born here. Why don't you take a train? You can go direct from Szolnok to Debrecen and put your bicycle in the baggage car.'

'Travelling through isn't the same as being born here.' Yet I could not explain why it was that I wanted to cross the Plain mile by mile. To her it was simply dull, and besides, the present heat wave was too much for a pale English person. I would boil like a chicken. She wrote down for me all the vocabulary I could possibly need for tickets and to register my bicycle as luggage.

When I left I hoped that I appeared to be going in the right direction for Szolnok.

Late in the afternoon I turned into a headwind, down a road that ran with unswerving direction through long fields of black plough and threatened to continue so for thirty miles. Storm clouds rose suddenly and swelled into a louring pewter sky, then shattered into stinging hail.

A few kilometres on, another bar gave sordid shelter. The regulars impassively looked over the newcomers the weather drove in – two motorcyclists and a group of gipsies besides myself. The place stank of beer and urine and damp clothes. I peered through the filthy window pane, ready to leave at the first thinning of the storm. An old man in a cloth cap looked over my shoulder and shook his head. He had a sad, hollow face, a long turkey neck with check shirt buttoned tight.

'It'll be a while yet.' He spoke German. 'Are you from Germany? I worked there once.'

'England.'

'D'you bike all the way?'

'Only from Vienna.'

'How many kilometres?'

I hadn't counted. 'I've been wandering about a bit, I don't quite know.'

His gloom deepened. 'So how many kilometres do you do a day? And how many days?'

'Anything between sixty and a hundred and twenty. But you see I stop a lot, look at places. I don't cycle all the time and some days I don't go anywhere.'

'Well you won't get far like that! Where are you planning to go?'

'Istanbul.'

'How far?'

'Two or three thousand kilometres. It depends which way I go.'

'That's a big difference, Miss. I'd think hard about that if I was you.' He changed the subject, in search of facts elsewhere. 'That your bike out there? English, isn't it? How much did it cost?'

I told him.

'That's a lot. You should have waited and bought one here.'

But it was a very lightweight bike, with many gears to make hills easy.

'How many gears?'

This was only the first of many such wayside conversations. Why were men so desperate to count everything? (Women, I later found, tended to ask quite different things such as where and why, and was I married then why no children and what did my husband think?) I was glad when he pointed outside again.

'There, it's brightening.'

I rode off as the rain stopped, along a steaming road. The sky widened as the last clouds slipped towards the horizon. When the sun set, a red sphere, it was perfectly clear.

The towns were little more than overgrown villages. Urban formality was provided by a few neo-classical façades, a touch of grandeur by a château-like town hall with dusty clipped hedges in front. The hotels were post-war, standard plan and generally empty; their restaurants were impersonal as canteens. In the restaurants music was obligatory, not the traditional gipsy violins but Hungarian rock from electric guitar, keyboard and drums. The local youth came nightly to drink beer and Coke. There was nowhere much else for them to go.

'They don't understand jazz,' moaned a modern-day gipsy musician, on contract for six months at the hotel in a manufacturing town. 'We play them a little every now and then, we think one day they will start to like it. But they get restless, ask for something else. No taste.'

He had come up to talk to me during the break between sets. He was self-consciously Western, smooth as if he was on celluloid. 'You're from Holland aren't you?'

I nodded.

'I can usually tell. You people all speak English, yuh? I learned my English when I did a contract in Norway. Beautiful place that, beautiful women . . . So you like my music?'

I nodded again.

'I saw you sitting there and knew what you'd like. We don't often get anyone here with taste. We played some stuff specially for you.'

'Thank you.'

'I wrote the songs too. Pity you can't understand the words.'

'Yes.'

The conversation lagged. The absence of music in the room was becoming noticeable. 'I think they want you back up there,' I said. 'Isn't it time you started the next set?'

'Yuh. See you later.'

When the music started again, I crept out. Maybe I should have spent the evening in the town cinema watching *Mad Max*.

The people of the Plain seemed heavy and slow. Flaccid, as if they lacked some tension that is born of a broken horizon.

I wandered off my route to the hot springs of Berekfürdő, enticed in the heat by road signs showing a swimmer cutting through waves. This village was different, from the first bungalow hemmed around by a cypress hedge and advertising bed-and-breakfast. It had a recognisable resort air, with children and fat men in swimming trunks queuing by ice-cream stalls. Except that their nudity seemed indecent without sea. Instead there was the hot brown water of the thermal bath (thirty-four to thirty-six degrees) filled with stout matrons, and the lukewarm brown water of the swimming pools. All through the thermal park, where sparse grass and pollarded chestnuts had to stand in for sand and striped umbrellas, big bronzed bodies lay splayed on coloured towels. Young women sunbathed nude out of sight on the roof of the treatment rooms; older women kept to deck chairs in the shade, deep in the pages of *Desirée* or some other fat fiction.

* * *

Further out to the east, the Hortobágy is the last great expanse of the Hungarian *puszta*, or wilderness. It is crossed by a road, partly drained and irrigated now, and the town of Hortobágy at its heart is a major tourist centre, famed for gipsy bands and *folklorique* displays. I did not go there, preferring to keep intact a childhood dream of horsemen. I skirted the *puszta* on side roads.

I bought breakfast in a village: a great round loaf glazed to a Rembrandt varnish, hot and white within the crust; butter and honey to go with it. I stopped on a grassy verge to eat, my back to a tree trunk, warmed by the slanting early sun. A gipsy cart trotted up, the driver absently singing, wife beside him, son astride sacks in the back. The moment they saw me they laughed, inexplicably, and laughed away into the distance.

Around midday I reached one of the drainage channels and rode up it into the blond grassland. The dyke was green and densely edged with rushes and shrubby acacias. The hard leaves of the rushes made a tinny rustling. I sat on a bridge in the thin shade of a willow. A rat swam across, snout out of the water, as emerald and sapphire dragon-flies wove through the air above. A heron wheeled over a branch of the dyke further off. All around was dry steppe; to the south it bleached out into a white rippling line. In other directions the line was crisper and varied by a hump of trees or the long shallow roof of a barn or farmhouse and the raised cross-pole of a well.

For minutes I watched a flock of sheep amble towards me. At first they seemed no more than a dappled puddle on the landscape, but then I could make out their round haunches white in the sun and the legs shadowy beneath. They moved in a reluctant, heaving mass, each leaning hard against the next as if intimidated by all the space around them, afraid of being separated by the slightest interval of air. The shepherd drove them on, grunting encouragement. As they passed over my bridge they made an extraordinary rumbling with their panting and pressing.

The shepherd greeted me curtly. He had the regular, fair looks and little moustache of the young Petőfi, the poet of the Plain, and he wore baggy trousers tucked into boots, a waistcoat with little silver buttons and a low-crowned black hat. So the old life of the Hortobágy had not quite vanished yet. He returned an hour later on the back of a friend's motorcycle, and they disappeared down a track, a puff of dust on the way to a remote farm.

I took a walk across the grass away from the dyke. Dry stalks scrunched underfoot, a flurry of crickets rose with every step and sometimes a partridge was put up with a dramatic whirr. I stopped and stretched out on the metallic, singing grass. Tiny things took on intensity. The earth, powdery and cracked, was furrowed by tracks and pitted with the burrows of small creatures. A bulbous-bodied spider, striped yellow and brown, raced greedily around a web where one cricket hung desiccating and another struggled feebly. I must have slept for a while.

When I woke, the white heat had gone from the day. Outlines and colours became more defined. Three deer got up and trotted away across now golden grass.

6

The Tisza cuts through the Plain from north to south; it rises in Carpathian Ruthenia, in what is now Russia, and ends in the Danube just above Belgrade, running through three countries now and touching a fourth – Romania – though its entire course was once contained within the kingdom of Hungary. For most of its length it is broad and lazy, mud-brown. Over the years it has left behind it odd snaking ponds where it once shifted its loose banks and a meander was cut off from the main stream. North of the Hortobágy the river takes in tributaries that run off the Bükk and Zemplén mountains and forms an indeterminate boundary to the Plain. At Tokaj it touches the southernmost outcrop of the Zemplén range, a lone blue hill which rises to a smooth-shouldered summit five hundred metres above the surrounding land.

I had to cross the river to reach the old town which lay at the base of the hill, coming along a dirt road past ponds where men sat in boats fishing, and waiting for the ferry to chug across from the opposite bank. The water was greener than before, clearer this far upstream.

Before turning south to Tokaj the Tisza runs through the remote district of the Nyírség. This is the north-eastern corner of Hungary, hemmed in on three sides by Czechoslovakia, Russia and Romania, and by the distant horseshoe of the Carpathians. It is a region of loess hills built of pale sand blown off the Plain. The river and its tributaries wander through the little valleys and damp hollows between the knolls. Much of the Nyírség was once swamp; this is said to have deterred the Turks from invading the area, which became a part of the autonomous principality of Transylvania. But perhaps they had no interest in the place: it has always been poor.

The peasants of the Nyírség are strong Calvinists, people with a tradition of independence that must have been encouraged by the knotted landscape where there would always have been somewhere to hide. It was they who first rose up at the end of the nineteenth century and voted to partition the land of their still feudal lords, some even marking out plots before the army came to brutally suppress the rebellion.

More was left of the past here than anywhere else I went in Hungary. Many of the villages had tiny Romanesque and Gothic churches where medieval frescoes had often survived under the Calvinist whitewash. And these churches were alive: the doors were open or else someone came with a key – unlike the locked and deserted yellow baroque churches of western Hungary.

Outside the church in Karcsa a man in baggy blue trousers scythed the verge. This door was already open. The building was very early, originally a circular church in the style of those of Dalmatia and the Adriatic coast; a nave had been tacked on later. The nave was dim, windowless on one side, but light filled the circle of the sanctuary. There were no images, no crosses, just white walls and the curves and shadowed planes of the vaulted ceiling. A round stone table, the top no more than two foot in diameter, stood in the centre of the sanctuary, the pattern of the pale brick floor radiating outwards from it. There were pews against the sanctuary walls as well as down the nave, and a simple wooden lectern for preaching. The pews were painted cornflower blue, with cushions of blue and white printed cotton; cloths of coarse white cotton embroidered in the same blue were draped over the fronts of the pews, over the lectern and the altar-table. Also on the table was a glass vase of tea roses, yellow and pink and thickly scented.

A tiny woman broke across the shaft of light at the doorway. She was dressed in black, with printed apron and kerchief. She looked fragile against the old oak of the door. She touched a pew, pointed out the arch that led into the sanctuary, resting on Tuscan columns of pinkish-grey stone; she raised a hand to shield her eyes from the light that came through the door behind her, nodded towards the carved capitals of the columns that supported the gallery. I went and looked. Amid swirling foliage rough carved figures like limp puppets threw up their arms and swivelled their heads back to look above them.

Erzsébet took me to her home beside the church, showed me the yard full of chickens and all the precious objects on the shelves in the parlour: a lamp with a green plastic shade which showed silhouetted fish when illuminated; a red plastic alarm clock; large boy and girl dolls that closed their eyes and squealed when they were turned upside down. All these were Russian, she said to impress me. Russia might have been a distant continent though we were no more than four or five miles from the Ukrainian border. From Germany she had a wooden barometer with figures that emerged from a Tyrolean doorway to denote fair and foul weather.

In the kitchen she made me coffee and fed me bread and salami, though she would have none herself. There were no Russian luxuries here, just a woodburning stove and a cold water tap. The shelves of the larder were already stocked with pickled summer vegetables, preserved cherries and puréed tomatoes in glass jars. She lived alone. Her husband and elder son were dead, her younger son worked in the industrial city of Miskolc: he came home every now and then. It was he who brought the foreign novelties.

In the next village I saw an old *kastély*, a manor in a stretch of parkland. The house, within a high-walled courtyard, had a single turret like a very minor French château. It had been restored but emptied of its original furnishings and filled instead with displays of folk art. The garden rather than the house preserved a memory of its history. A path led into a wood where my feet fell softly on a deep bed of leaves and small green frogs jumped aside as I walked. It ended in a clearing where there was a pond and a wooden boathouse whose roof, ogee-arched and ornamented with iron finials, drooped low towards the water.

It was strange how few traces of the past were left in the places I travelled through. I had seen a handful of other manors on the way. Most were nineteenth-century houses on the typical Eastern European plan: a long single-storey building in pink or ochre stucco with wings jutting out to enclose a courtyard on two sides, and neo-classical pediment and pilasters at the entrance – the houses of the Russian rural gentry had been similar, though made of wood. Now they were either derelict, with the courtyard given over to farm machinery or the collective's stores, or they had been roughly converted into schools and institutions.

I crossed the Tisza again on a ferry. It was narrower now, yet still boys stood astride bicycles watching from the embankment as others swam from willow-hung beaches, so many heads dotted across the water.

In Ricse I stopped for a Coca-Cola. In front of the bar, at a fork in the road, was a stone fountain like a futuristic gravestone with spouts jutting dry over an empty trough. It was engraved: Julius somebody or other, July 1926, New York. An emigrant villager made good, I guessed. Was the fountain a beneficent gesture made in his will? Probably not, or there would have been two dates, for birth and death. More likely he had swaggered in one summer and had the fountain built to remind his old drinking companions of his exceptional fortune. I did not imagine anyone would have returned to Ricse for long, time enough only for a welcome party and a send-off again to the New World.

There were just two men in the bar, an old Hungarian and a gipsy. The Hungarian had lost the top two joints from most of the fingers of his left hand. The gipsy was huge and dark, with long arms that dangled almost to his knees; he asked where I was from. '*Polska? Bolgár?*'

'*Angol.*'

He winked slowly and deliberately. I could not see any special significance in the fact that I was English. Irritated, I began to interrogate him in pidgin Hungarian. Where did he work?

In Budapest.

It was Monday, so why was he not there?

He pouted, raised his glass and winked again.

Many of his people lived in the Nyírség. Since the war the gipsies of Hungary have been forced to settle. Now, though spread throughout the country, the population is concentrated in the poorest areas where houses – if not jobs – are easiest to come by. For work they travel to the cities. I had been told of the 'Black Train' which left Budapest's Eastern Station every Friday evening carrying the gipsy men back to their families in the Nyírség for the weekend. I asked this man about his family.

He said he had many, many children, and down went the eyelid again.

The Hungarian interrupted. 'Nine. He has nine children.' He held up his stumps and fingers for me to count.

I came to the Tisza for the last time in the rain, down a track that had been turned to thick mud by the downpour so that the bicycle wheels caked solid and I was forced to walk. The bank itself was a steep mud-slide where I could barely keep my grip as I cupped my hands and shouted across to the ferry mooring on the opposite side.

The river was black and the rain stabbed it with silver points. The rain fell with a metallic patter that was drowned at moments by thunder. There was no shelter; I could only stand and yell until two figures at last appeared, one large, one small, and picked their way crab-like down the bank the other side to start the ferry moving. It had no engine and was wound slowly across the water along a steel rope. I slithered on, helped by a ferryman in black oilskins and enormous sou'wester; the smaller figure was that of his son, who held a mac over his head and quickly looked me over before taking the only shelter on the metal raft, beneath the winch hood.

I tipped them both extravagantly and was invited to wait out the rest of the storm in their hut on the other bank. In an impenetrable silence the ferryman offered me an armchair in a neat waiting room, before a low table with a pot of artificial flowers, and left me there like royalty. Father and son sat hunched on the lower bed of a bunk in the adjoining room and watched me through the open door.

It was to rain almost continuously for two days, though the storm soon lost its intensity. Moving by will, enfolded in waterproofs, I felt cut off from the grey villages I passed through. I stopped little, only to snatch a picnic lunch beneath an oak tree or to visit a church. One – small, Gothic, whitewashed – had rain-soaked larches pressing up against it, and a wooden belfry alongside that thrust a thin spire into cloud. Another was set in a plum orchard where water dripped from the trees on to ground that was covered in fallen fruit. The smell of the plums filled the little church. The walls had been gaily painted in the seventeenth century in a leafy pattern in russet and blue, with a rough inscription in Latin giving the date and the name of the pastor, but older frescoes survived in the sanctuary and low on the walls of the nave: sloe-eyed figures of evangelists and early saints. The caretaker identified each one. Her eyes watched my face for signs of appreciation. '*Fantasztikus?*'

'Yes. *Fantasztikus.*' A white-bearded Peter, John, Cosmas and Damian, Saint Helena and a faded nativity. Byzantium had influenced the style as well as the choice of saints; this church was close to the edge of Gothic Europe.

Her dog had come in with us, a shaggy black animal, and padded around the church before settling to doze at the foot of the gallery staircase. She talked to me of the Reformation as if it had happened within living memory and explained that though the church was now Protestant, the pictures had been painted by Catholics. 'And you, what are you in England?'

I told her that my family was Catholic though most of the English were Protestant, and that the old paintings on our churches had almost all been whitewashed over.

We walked back through the orchard. She pointed at a heavily laden branch that had come down in the storms of the past few days. 'Look at the fruit on it. Such a year!' But at least the bruised plums would be good for *pálinka*, the Hungarian plum brandy. The fruit seemed to be fermenting where it lay, so strong was the scent in the air.

When she saw my bicycle at the gate she turned in alarm. 'You came by bicycle? Alone? You are not afraid?'

No, I said, I had travelled a long way.

'But there is danger. Gipsies!' She made a vicious stabbing gesture that said clearly how a gipsy would think nothing of putting a knife into me and taking all I had: it was the traditional warning of the Hungarian peasant.

7

I went again on to the Plain and south to Debrecen, from where I was to cross into Romania.

I longed to see the Carpathians. I would have been glad to see any mountains rise after so much flatness but the Carpathians were the most mysterious mountains in Europe. I once read a story by Conrad about a Carpathian peasant who sold his patrimony for a future in America but was instead shipwrecked on a flat stretch of English coast. To the lowland English who met him he was extraordinary, too exotic; they feared him for the mountain-born ease with which he vaulted stiles and crossed their tame fields, and for the passion in the alien words he spoke. His striding figure stayed in my mind long after. In the story it was not clear exactly where he came from, some unnamed valley in the eastern Carpathians. In Conrad's time these were a remote district of Austro-Hungary; today most of the Carpathian range falls within the borders of Romania.

I was getting a little afraid of Romania. That country was said to have the most repressive government in Eastern Europe. A Stalinist climate of fear was said to prevail there: one person in three a police informer, children taught to spy on their parents, quiet beatings and disappearance of dissidents. The president, Ceauşescu, was compared with Papa Doc, Marcos and the madder African dictators. Surprisingly little information had been available in England, yet even the official advice for tourists was ominous. It stated that contact between citizens and foreigners was restricted: all conversations with foreigners were to be reported to the police within twenty-four hours, and no foreigners were to be given a place to stay or even a place to camp.

The implications of all this had sunk deeper the longer I spent in Hungary. At first it had been easy to disregard jokes about shortages of salami and light bulbs. Among the fierce nationalisms of Eastern and Central Europe there is an old prejudice against the Romanians, who are seen as Latin and subtle, accused of spinelessness, laziness, even 'Byzantine whorishness'; Bismarck once gave voice to it: 'I care for the Romanians as I do for my glass once it is empty.' But I could not ignore the vehemence with which Hungarians spoke about the poverty of the country, which was bankrupt now despite its natural richness in oil, minerals and land: 'The people are starving. They will steal from you to feed themselves. And the police are brutes. Do not imagine that your British passport will protect you there.'

In Budapest I received reassurance from a British diplomat who knew the region. 'I envy you,' he said. 'It will be like cycling through the fourteenth century. Though you realise you may be followed?' he added. 'I wonder whether the *Securitate* have bicycles.'

I thought it funny, sitting there in the Embassy. 'I should be able to lose them quickly on a Dawes Galaxy.'

'In that case, perhaps a very slow black limousine.' But then he remembered his position. 'Don't quote me of course if you get kidnapped or anything.'

'No, no, of course not.'

Debrecen was the Plain's capital, a market town that centred on a broad thoroughfare done up with turn-of-the-century swagger. It was American in its main-streetness, directly evolved from those villages ribboning along the level roads. Historically the town was a Calvinist stronghold, and the neo-classical Great Church that stood in the middle of the thoroughfare was uncompromisingly Protestant with its dark lines of pews set before a pulpit as before a judge's bench: a place for plain men to talk straight to God.

It was still a thriving town, with the best food shops I saw in all Hungary: windows strung with red and black salamis, piled with giant jars of pickled cucumbers; steaming steel vats of stuffed cabbage and goulash in the self-service restaurants. Peasants came far to the great covered market. Some piled on the trestle tables lush heaps of tomatoes, paprikas, melons, plums and peaches. Beside them, lone grey-haired men and women stood amateurishly before a few jars of honey of different colours and thicknesses, a basket of eggs or bags of yellow home-made noodles. Others brought bunches of dried thyme and fennel; a heap of wild mushrooms; curd cheeses in muslin; or deep red chillies which they threaded on strings. By the entrance old women like Erzsébet tried to catch the eye with gaudy bunches of garden flowers, marigolds, achillea and dahlias. I went to the market early on a damp morning before I left, bought a whole salami and what few token rations would fit into a bicycle pannier. For breakfast I had strong coffee and at least two flaking, cherry-filled strudels: I doubted I would find anything so good over the border.

In Debrecen I had had news from England. A report had appeared in the papers there that the demolition of villages had begun in Transylvania. (It turned out later that this report was false.) I wondered whether I really wanted to go there. I did not want to blunder on to some churned-up patch of earth where a village had once been, nor to take snapshots of someone else's tragedy. But it was almost too easy to cross the border. The notorious immigration and customs officials were deliberately obstructive with everyone else. The only other Western Europeans who attempted to enter the country, a Mediterranean and seedy French couple who belonged by some bar in a Jean Gabin movie, turned furiously back into Hungary with screams of '*Putains! Bêtes! Quels animaux, sces Romains . . .*' I do not know what drove them to such disgust. My journey was treated by the officials as a huge joke; they left off their searches and interrogations, left Hungarians and Romanians standing in the drizzle beside turned-out suitcases, cardboard boxes and plastic bags, came to count the gears on my bicycle and wish me *bon voyage*. I was glad that they spoke French, and that Romanian sounded so easy after Hungarian; it was unmistakably a Latin language despite odd word-endings and Slavonic borrowings.

It was fourteen kilometres into the town of Oradea. Almost immediately the fields were lost and the road entered a grey industrial inferno. A huge pipeline snaked alongside, part lagged, part rusting, heaved up at points to bridge the entrance to a factory that would have looked derelict but for the smoke that seeped from its chimneys. Overhead, strands of stinking smoke, white, grey, brown, hung still and almost horizontal beneath leaden clouds. There were signs along the road, red with white lettering: PACE CEAUŞESCU; PARTIDUL COMUNIST ROMĂN; ROMANIA COMUNISM: CEAUŞESCU EROISM.

Grey apartment blocks became interspersed with the factories and gradually replaced them, then came to an end suddenly before a hill and a park and the baroque Bishop's Palace, with behind it the elegant concave front of the Roman Catholic cathedral, bright ochre yellow even in the rain. The centre of Oradea was frivolously Austro-

Hungarian. Its Ruritanian architecture culminated in extravagant Secessionist apartment houses that had rippling gables and sugar-caster turrets, stuccoed in pink and turquoise and studded with coloured tiles and ceramic rosettes.

The hotel I found in the Strada Republicii had a sign in angular 1930s lettering: HOTEL vertical to the left of the doorway; PARC, ill-spaced, cutting across horizontally from just below the 'T'. The doors themselves were a wonderful black tangle of art-nouveau ironwork. The reception desk was built in behind glass and dark panelling at the base of a stairwell that was lit only by a stained-glass skylight high above.

'A room? Yes, we have many rooms.' The girl at the desk in the dimness there shook off her sleepiness. 'What sort of room would you like?'

'Just a room. A bed. Perhaps a view of the street?'

I told her how I liked the look of the town, how it was not at all what I had expected. She said it was newly restored, then giggled, looked from side to side and added, 'But some people say they've turned it into a cookie!'

'How do you mean?'

'Look at the stairs.'

The plaster frieze above the staircase depicted dragonflies and water-lilies thickly painted in the gaudy colours of a child's paintbox. I said I liked it.

'You don't think it's a little . . . strident?'

'Perhaps. I'm not sure I could live with it. In England people might say it was vulgar.'

'Vulgar. That's the word! We say the same in Romanian: *vulgar*.'

She gave me the key to my room and showed me another one. 'This is the key to the bathroom. You can come down here and get it anytime, and you must pay fourteen *lei*. But you will not want one.'

'Why not?'

'The water is cold.'

'Always?'

'On Mondays and Fridays.'

'Oh. Why's that?'

'Economy.' She giggled again. 'For economy, in all of Oradea we have no hot water on Mondays or Fridays.'

*   *   *

I went for a walk. It was strange to see the smoking chimneys of the industrial town at the end of the sugary streets. The drizzle had stopped and the clouds began to dissolve. Under pools of blue sky the town became a set for an operetta. The Strada Republicii was paved in concentric white circles like the floor of a stage, on which a choreographed chorus strolled and loitered, while soldiers leant against walls and eyed the girls. A young couple stood on the bridge and looked down the river, where the silver dome of the synagogue was reflected in the water. A group of peasants seemed to have strayed into the wrong scene and wandered down an art-nouveau arcade, men in wide-brimmed felt hats and dark stick-on moustaches. In the town square a gaunt policeman observed the passers-by, swishing a rubbery baton in his hand.

But too often people's faces looked sullen and blank. Collectively they had an ashen look that goes with hunger and poverty, a look common enough in the third world but rare on the faces of Europeans. They were physically smaller than the Hungarians. And I noticed among them a disproportionate number of drunks with leering, watery stares, hovering on the edge of the pavement or stumbling down the streets. This was not just my preconceptions speaking; this country was visibly different.

I thought at first that all the shops were shut. It was five or six o'clock and they looked dark inside. But as people went in and out I realised that they were in fact open, just unlit. For economy. There was a long queue outside a greengrocer's but hardly anyone in the supermarket, down the aisles of identical glass jars whose generally colourless contents were described by monotonous labels: cucumbers, peas, carrots, peas and carrots mixed, cabbage, spinach, apricots, apples, pears, pear jam, apricot jam. I could find nothing I wanted and carried my empty plastic basket back past the check-out girl in the hygienic white headscarf and overall, past a sign that seemed to be a warning for shoplifters. (The first such sign I had seen in a Socialist country, though there did not seem to be much worth stealing.)

I tried to buy a Romanian dictionary. There were lots of bookshops in Oradea, and I went to almost every one. Their layout was as monotonous as that of the supermarkets, their contents little more varied, though customers peered closely at the spines of books on the obscure shelves at the back. At the front, in the light of the window, were the works of Ceauşescu. These thick volumes of historical and political pronouncements in de-luxe bindings occupied, at a guess, about a sixth of the shelf space in each shop – a predominance roughly equivalent to that of pickled cucumbers in the supermarkets. Foreign literature was limited to collected works of Goethe, Byron, Flaubert and modern Soviet poets. There was no English–Romanian dictionary available, nor a French–Romanian one, though German, Polish, Serbo-Croat and, curiously, Dutch were in good supply.

As I went on through Romania, I was to find the same books time and again, though I was occasionally surprised to hit a patch of Lytton-Strachey, Montesquieu or Boccaccio in an unlikely town. I never did find an English–Romanian or even a French–Romanian dictionary. I had to make do with a French phrasebook produced by the state publishing house; in spare moments I broke down the extraordinarily useless phrases into their component parts and constructed a rough guess at a dictionary from them. It was all a question of what chanced to be in print. A typesetter I met explained that there was a severe paper shortage: Romania's own paper mills produced only lavatory paper and newsprint – she said in practice these two products might as well have been interchangeable anyway – and as there was no hard currency for the import of other quality papers, economies were made on book production. She had had no work to do for the previous five months.

At night the streets were dark. For economy, only one street lamp in three was illuminated, casting an isolated pool of light. As I went back from a restaurant to the hotel a man came up quietly beside me and spoke in French.

'*Pardon, mais est-ce-que vous êtes française?*'

'*Non.*'

'*Mais vous parlez français?*' He and his friends had seen me in the restaurant and it seemed that, as the best French-speaker, he had been sent to come and invite me to meet them. He did so with old-fashioned courtesy. We stopped beneath the next street lamp and introduced ourselves. His name was Nicolae. He was a small man in his mid-thirties, with a flat, boxer's face and the clothes of a jazz musician: striped shirt roughly tucked into checked trousers. He apologised that he spoke only French; some of his friends knew English. They were intellectuals, and some were artists; perhaps I would like to see their work. But most of all he was sorry that his wife was away; she was a teacher of English but had never had a chance to speak with a native.

59

Later I learnt his story, which was not an unusual one. His wife and three children, aged between six and ten, were in West Germany. His wife's mother was an ethnic German, though born in Romania, and because of this she had been granted a permit to take the children to visit relatives in Germany. They were not going to return. He would apply for permission to join them instead. He hoped that this would come through in a couple of years' time. Until then he would not see them at all. '*C'est triste, mais c'est nécessaire.*' Necessity figured largely in his talk: the necessity of giving the children some opportunity, of getting them out of Romania, the necessity of living in a certain way, even of getting drunk.

Only three-fifths of the population of Transylvania are Romanian. Members of the ethnic minorities – of which the two million Hungarians and four hundred thousand Germans are the largest groups – have a theoretical right to leave and in the present climate most seem to be trying to do so. In 1987, an estimated ten thousand refugees sought political asylum in Hungary, and a similar number in 1988; of these probably half left officially, half simply failed to return from visits to relatives. An unknown number cross the border illegally. There have been a few reports of people being shot by border guards; it is likely that far more are caught and find their way to prison instead. In one Transylvanian town I met an ethnic Hungarian who had just spent six months behind bars after his third try for Hungary; he looked frayed and seedy and had no expectation of work: next time, he said, he would make a try for Yugoslavia. Some people have fled to Bulgaria, some even to the Soviet Union.

Around eleven thousand people of German race are permitted to leave each year to settle in West Germany. It is reported that the West German government pays Bucharest a lump sum for each one – as much as ten thousand deutschmarks (£3,300) per working adult, four thousand per child and six thousand per pensioner – and that Israel likewise pays for Jews allowed to leave. Other exit visas have been bartered in return for trade agreements and Western favour.

Emigration may be good business; it may also be an effective safety-valve, disposing of potential Romanian dissidents as well as slowly reducing the problems of the minorities. However the government is reluctant to see so many go, and all the more so when industrial expansion and a declining birth-rate have caused breeding to be regarded as a citizen's patriotic duty – encouraged by such measures as prohibition of abortion on all grounds, tax laws penalising childless couples and compulsory gynaecological examinations for married women of child-bearing age if they do not quickly become pregnant. Would-be emigrants are often harassed from the day they put their papers in, and their relatives may suffer when they are gone. In 1982, only foreign outrage prevented the imposition of an 'education tax' on emigrants, by which they would have to pay the state back before they left the country for all the education they had received. Payments were to be made in hard currency, at rates that ran into thousands of dollars. It was not explained how this was to be achieved when Romanian citizens were not permitted to possess foreign currency anyway.

Nicolae's flat was off a courtyard in a nineteenth-century apartment house. The two rooms were white and high-ceilinged, with a few pieces of Viennese furniture, a grand piano, an armoire and a tarnished mirror in a curling mahogany frame – inherited things; his family were old Romanian bourgeoisie. There was a vase of dried wild flowers at the window, and on the walls were paintings by friends. Although his wife and children had been gone only a few weeks, there was already a film of desertion on the flat, dust and overflowing ashtrays and unplumped cushions.

Two of his friends from the restaurant were already there. They welcomed me with the same old-fashioned continental manners. Károly was brown, wiry, impish, somehow Italian in his expressiveness and delicacy of movement. He was an artist and made fine, delicate drawings. He loved the Renaissance and wanted to know, had I been to Florence and Siena? Had I seen Giotto's frescos in Assisi, or those of Piero della Francesca at Arezzo? He knew only poor reproductions. And how about Dante; had I read Dante?

György looked German by contrast, with a fleshy blond handsomeness. His clothes were crisp and new, and looked as though they had been sent from abroad; his fiancée was already in Hungary, and he expected his papers to come through soon. Hungary he considered as just a springboard; he saw their future in West Germany. He seemed sure, practical, unhesitating. He was not an artist but a doctor. And because he was a doctor he could make us happy for the evening with a bottle of plum brandy. He told me cynically that doctors were not highly regarded in Romania. They were paid less than workers.

Workers thought themselves superior as a result, until they were ill; then they came to the surgery with flattery and a packet of American cigarettes to make up for it. Peasants brought the plum brandy they made. When they were cured, they despised the doctors all the more for accepting their gifts. Such were the rewards for a professional in Romania.

I stayed a couple of days in Oradea. In that time I came strangely close to the three of them. Travelling alone you can form swift friendships and this one caught me off balance: I had been in the country only a few hours and had barely worked out the units of currency before we met. That first evening I poured out my relief at the fear they had instantly dispelled; I had had a sneaking worry that people would be reluctant even to tell me the way lest they should have to report to the police afterwards. On the other hand, I was afraid that I might unwittingly cause problems for those people who were friendly to me. The response was immediate on this point: to accept what people chose to give; it was their right to offer hospitality, as well as their tradition.

In a surge of sympathy that was inspired by their own confidences I also told them more about myself than I had intended to tell anyone in Romania. The sensible course in a country that keeps itself so close is to play the innocent tourist, not to show too much interest in politics or admit involvement in writing. But I was not used to concealment; I needed to trust people who seemed to trust me. There was silence when I had answered their question about what I did for a living, as if nobody had heard.

It took a while to realise that there were subtle taboos in operation even when people seemed to speak openly. Individuals told me far more when we were alone than when their friends were around; and sometimes I guessed that what appeared to be a misunderstanding in the language we spoke was actually evasion. I was a brash Westerner among these undercurrents. I am not sure that I understand now what was or was not behind what people said. Only I came to feel that caution was second nature here; that friendships were made and carried on in the awareness that one might be overheard or informed upon.

My indiscretion may have encouraged them to tell me more, for certainly they tried hard to make me understand the place they lived in. Perhaps they would have done so anyway: tourist or writer, I was a representative of the outside world and Romanians wanted the world to know. Early in our conversation, they asked what I knew of the situation in Transylvania – though Nicolae was ethnically Romanian and the others Hungarian, all three came from towns in the Carpathians and identified themselves as Transylvanian. They asked what I understood of the problems of the minorities, both Hungarian and German; and if we in England knew of the threat to the villages. On this last question I said that there had been much in the papers about it but that all our news came via Hungary, never direct: was the threat real? They shrugged. Most of their information also came from Hungary, from news broadcasts on radio and television. They said only that they hoped it was no more than an idea. Before, Ceauşescu had had great notions that had come to nothing; let us hope that this was one of them. But they spoke without conviction. Too many of his notions did take shape.

György broke the gloom. Did I have any Scottish blood? For Transylvania and Scotland, he believed, had much in common: highland landscapes and castles with hunting trophies on the walls; a wild history of peasants and barons and a yen for independence. Under the Romans, Dacian regiments had been sent to man Hadrian's Wall. And then, too, there were the ballads and the dances. Had I ever danced a *csárdás* or heard a Transylvanian song?

Nicolae went to the piano and played while the others sang, sad, romantic ballads in Hungarian, then racing dance tunes to which they clapped their hands. György took the glass of plum brandy from me, pulled me from the chair and began to teach me the steps of a *csárdás*.

'You know the difference between a Transylvanian and a Romanian song? The Transylvanian song is melodious, emotional; but the Romanian song is all thumping and stamping. It is the song of the peasant. Niki, play us a Romanian song!'

Nicolae pounded one off the piano. And the Hungarians teased him for it. They joked that his broad, flat-nosed face was that of a peasant. He took it in good humour but slipped into a different tune; suddenly I realised it was 'My Bonny Lies Over the Ocean'. I was ashamed that they, not I, knew all the words.

The next day I took it easy, wandered round the town, found the Hotel Dacia with the hard-currency store where special goods were supposed to be available for tourists. I wanted to buy a bottle of Scottish whisky for Nicolae and the others, but there were no tourists and few imports apart from coffee and Hungarian salami, which were bought with black-market dollars by Romanians who could not obtain them elsewhere. It was Saturday so I went back to the Hotel Parc and had a hot bath. Then dozed away the last of a hangover with the windows open and the curtains blowing, to the sound of the afternoon strollers on the street outside.

It was a good hotel room; the high ceiling and crumbling cornice made up for the damp that spread beneath the basin and for the lone, dripping cold-water tap. Best was its position overlooking the Strada Republicii. Opposite, I looked down another street that ran past the opera house, a long straight street that cut through the centre of the town. As I leant at the window Károly strolled up and when he reached the junction I waved to him. I joined him for an ersatz coffee and a small square of stale cake at the café on the corner. I said it was Mediterranean, the crowds walking in the sun. Not for him, he answered. He did not like to listen to their talk.

Why? What did they say?

It was not what they said but that they laughed only on the surface. He knew how they felt underneath.

Could he not close his eyes, allow himself a fantasy?

No, he said. But we could have a drink.

The afternoon trailed into evening in the noisy beer garden round the back of the Hotel Parc. I met a sample of the town's intellectuals: a couple of professors, the curator of the Ady Endre Museum, the man who ran the collective shop where artists and craftspeople sold their work. I asked him how he priced items, be they paintings, one-off dresses or jewellery. 'It's very easy,' he told me. 'Artists get paid according to their qualifications and status. Sometimes things sell, sometimes they don't. How do you do it in England?

I explained that prices were supposed to reflect talent but in practice had more to do with demand and fashion; though at the lower end of the crafts market they would be based on the cost of raw materials.

'But not on the qualifications or experience of the maker? That does not sound very fair to me.'

Károly became more taut and bright as he drank. It was surprising that such brilliance could come from the cloudy Romanian beer. He suddenly got up and said we should find György and led me off down darkening streets. He hummed a little tune. 'This song is one you should know; we learned it in school:

I'm glad to be born in Romania,
I'm glad to be drinking in Romania . . .'

At György's house we met a slight, blonde woman who called up to him and the three of us waited in the street until he came down. The next-door house was being rebuilt and in its courtyard was a neat pile of bricks. Károly sneaked in and chose one brick with great care. He gave it to me.

'Here, take this.'

'Thanks. What is it?'

'A brick.'

'I can see that.'

'A brick from the building of Socialism.'

'Sshh. You're drunk.' The woman, Nina, took the brick and put it back on top of the pile.

We all went to Nicolae's. There was little to do in Oradea but go to Nicolae's. Hungarian television was showing a recording of a charity pop concert which had taken place in the West earlier in the year. (They said they never watched Romanian television: programmes, which lasted only a few hours a day, generally alternated between Ceauşescu's interminable speeches and something called *Telejurnal*. *Telejurnal* showed everyday life in happy factories and agricultural collectives where production quotas were always exceeded and where Ceauşescu regularly came to shake hands with the workers.)

A couple of people from the beer garden came round and we drank sour, watery wine the colour of cider. A man called Teodorescu sat deep in an armchair and drained glass after glass. He was in his fifties, older than the others, dark, thin-faced, with a long nose and thin moustache. He wore a beige-coloured suit, a spotted red tie and a white shirt that bulged open, unbuttoned, as he got drunk. He talked to me in affected, over-accented French; he told me he had been to France just after the war, and he seemed to think this a qualification for monopolising me. Such a pity I had not come to his house that evening; he had a colour television – as if only he and I were cosmopolitan enough to appreciate such things. But, he joked, black-and-white was good enough for this programme; who needed to see Harry Belafonte, Ray Charles, Michael Jackson in colour? '*Les nègres*,' he sneered. '*Connaissez-vous les nègres? Ils puent.*' When I disagreed he said he was sure he knew more about them than I; he had been to north Africa and there he had known negro women. '*Elles puent comme des bêtes.*' His Byzantine nose wrinkled.

Others besides myself seemed to find him offensive, but for some reason they tolerated him there. A child came in, Nina's son – they too were waiting to leave; his father was already in the West. He was a shy, dark boy of nine or ten. Teodorescu told him to play some music for us. He turned the television down and sat the boy at the piano, then stood there as the boy nervously began to play. When he hit a wrong note Teodorescu exclaimed, stopped him, told him to go back to the beginning. György interrupted, took the boy to find his mother in another room; he looked tense with anger but said nothing to Teodorescu.

I went out for a walk and Nicolae joined me. All the televisions in Oradea must have been tuned to the concert: Stevie Wonder sang behind art-nouveau windows. There was no lighting at all on the smaller streets. The darkness made it beautiful: the stars and the almost full moon were far clearer than you ever expect to see them from within a town and the lit windows glowed yellow. Nicolae mentioned places he thought I should see. He knew the country well, never having been out of it. He gave me the addresses of a few friends I could contact. But he asked me not to tell them, or anyone at the flat, what he had said to me about where his wife was; as far as they knew she was somewhere else, not in Germany.

We got back as the concert on television ended. Teodorescu had left. Somebody switched to the Romanian channel. Preparations were going on in Arad, where Ceauşescu was to meet the Hungarian premier, Károly Grosz, the following day for talks on Transylvania.

'What will happen?' I asked.

'A monologue,' Károly replied. 'Poor Mr Grosz.'

President Ceauşescu and his wife Elena were shown on their way to Arad, passing through great crowds waving Romanian flags. György said that they got the day off from work to go and cheer. 'What do you think of our imperial family?'

'Ceauşescu looks older than in the pictures I've seen.'

'Well, this is real life.'

I had seen a picture of Ceauşescu at home, the frontispiece to a book called *Nicolae Ceauşescu: Fighter for Détente, Disarmament and Peace*. The book was given to me at the Romanian Consulate in London when I went to collect my visa. There was a hitch, I had to negotiate with an official on the number of days, and then wait while he disappeared through mahogany double doors to find the correct stamps. I browsed the yellowing pamphlets on the table in the entrance hall – the Consulate was in a grey nineteenth-century villa close to Kensington Palace. And the doorman, or the man I assumed was the doorman, handed me the book: 'Please take this. It is my book.'

'You wrote it?'

'Yes.' He nodded decorously, a dark shadow of a man and no longer just a doorman. The blurb on the jacket did say that the author lived and worked in London, though the text reeked of bad translation.

It was unreadable of course, a hagiography. Which was why I got little further than the frontispiece. This was a hand-coloured photograph of the Romanian president: a smooth-featured Latin face fleshy in middle-age; dark, curling hair tinged with grey; straight nose, brown eyes and pink lips twisted in a posed smile. The attempt at oily charm, the glimpse of a boldly patterned tie below the thick neck, and the hand-colouring itself, recalled publicity shots of third-rate Italian tenors and Indian film stars. You could almost smell the hair oil.

On television, the 'Greatest Son of the Romanian People' looked thinner, greyer, no more imposing than a provincial mayor. His wife, Comrade Academician Doctor Engineer Elena Ceauşescu, member of the Romanian equivalent to the Politburo, deputy prime minister and 'Greatest Daughter of the Romanian People', was a plain, mean-faced woman with a spinster's bun and a boxy suit that had an ornate brooch pinned to the collar.

György and I went into the kitchen and ate slices of bread and paprika bacon (poor man's salami, white fat with a hot dusting of paprika) with cauliflower pickle. György told me they rarely saw real salami. 'We say here that to see a full refrigerator you must first connect it to the TV set. The picture will then come on with the light when you open the door. But what is that to Ceauşescu? Ceauşescu says that the Romanian people will grow strong on bread and onions.'

'He's an old man now,' I said. 'Surely he can't last much longer?'

'He is seventy, but he could live to be ninety, like his father. Then there's his wife and then his son.'

Ceauşescu had been slowly increasing his power as leader of

Romania since 1965. By 1988 he had many members of the family in government with him, including one of Elena's brothers as a deputy prime minister and two of his own brothers in the Ministries of the Interior and Defence; his younger son Nicu was already a member of the Central Committee and some people said that Nicu was lined up to succeed his father.

'They are like . . .' György paused, frustrated at his inadequate English. He said it was the name of an animal he wanted.

'Lions?'

'No, not lions. Animals we have here, in the mountains.'

'Wolves?'

'Wolves. And we, we are the small animals in the forest.' He hunched his shoulders, shrinking into himself. He looked suddenly vulnerable. When I left, I hugged him. The last thing he said was 'Remember the tragedy of Transylvania.'

Tragedy was a melodramatic word. I walked back to the Hotel Parc. In the pink tower of the town hall the clock chimed twelve and tinkled a silly tune. It seemed an invitation to disbelieve.

In the morning I went to Nicolae's for breakfast, a Romanian breakfast of coffee and vermouth. Nicolae and Nina walked with me to the edge of the old town where the road to Cluj started, by a bridge over the river. It was a bright morning. They said I would reach the Carpathians by early afternoon.

8

I rode up the valley of the Criş Repede towards the great horseshoe of the Carpathians. On either side soft green hills came closer, striped with vines or humped with dark patches of deciduous woods; up ahead the hills were blue and long-backed. The air was clear after the week's rains and sun varnished the broad blades of the maize leaves.

A bicycle whirred alongside mine. Then another, and another. A fleet of five racing bicycles, Russian-made Sputniks, ridden by teenage boys in brightly coloured T-shirts and cycling shorts, with peaked caps turned backwards to shield the neck.

'Hi! You speak English?'

'I am English.'

The one who spoke was a lanky fair-haired boy. The others kept in a shy cluster behind us. It was the Oradea Cycling Club on a Sunday outing.

'My name is Stefan. What's yours?'

I told him.

'You understand what I say?'

'Yes. Your English is very good.'

'I have lessons two times a week. But I've never spoken with a British person before. I'm going to America. To New York.' His narrow face was alive with excitement.

'When?'

'Soon. Very soon. October maybe. My Dad's been there since last year. He's been sending me videos and tapes.'

'You mean you've got your papers?'

They had got the papers that said their papers were coming through.

'Are you looking forward to it?'

'You bet!'

I told him the cycling was safer in Romania: in thirty kilometres that morning I had been passed by only a handful of cars and trucks.

'In New York I guess they all have cars.'

I said some people still had bikes. I had heard about cycle couriers who stripped their bikes as for track racing, even of the brakes, and careered through central Manhattan without so much as stopping for a traffic light. In emergencies all a rider could do was grab the front wheel with his hand.

'Wow!' He translated to his friends.

We rode another few miles together but I could see them starting to fret at my pace; they would slowly gain on me then glide until they had dropped behind, then come up again. At last Stefan said they would go on ahead. He wished me luck.

'Good luck in New York!'

In the villages it was clearly Sunday. People sat still and upright on benches outside their houses, greeting anyone who came by along the road. From a walled courtyard on the edge of one village came the sound of a fiddle and of dancing.

Most of the traffic was horse-drawn, open carts or covered waggons. The few cars that passed were mainly those of Polish tourists but occasionally an international truck swept by, driving the carts on to the verge. Here and there a couple of waggons had stopped; the drivers sprawled on the ground while the horses grazed. Twice in the morning I saw on the road the same two hitchhikers, students from Leipzig with blond pony-tails and faded orange dungarees; they told me they were going to Făgăraş – the highest range in the southern Carpathians – and pronounced the word with the hippy reverence that Western students used to give to Nepal.

The arms of the valley closed on either side, the hills becoming steeper and more jagged. The climb to Piatra Craiului was not so hard as I had feared – I had never cycled in mountains before. At the top I bought a bottle of beer and lay triumphant in a field looking out to the jostling hills beyond. Village families also lazed on the grass, sending their children off down a white rocky track to play in the woods. Most were still dressed for church, the women wearing full skirts and stiff, tight jackets of sober blue-printed cotton, fine black aprons decorated with coloured braids, and ballooning white blouses. They spoke Hungarian, and the costume itself had the puritanical look of eastern Hungary.

I spent the night in a ski cabin a little way off the main road. The early morning had a chill in it that spurred me out to walk up the mountain behind. I could hear the sound of the river and of carts on the rough road at the base of the valley. High up along the track I took were dotted the houses of a scattered village, simple, single-storey cottages that were painted in soft colours: faded lavender and delphinium blues or a rosy pink. In the gardens were hollyhocks and touch-me-nots and bright yellow daisies, and vines trained along the fences. Up beyond the houses I padded through a beech wood, then came out on to an alpine meadow where the sun was now hot and the crickets sang and light fell sharply across the haystacks, defining each fine dry blade of mountain grass and wildflower stem.

Before Huedin the road dropped a little and the Carpathians began to stretch and smooth into the rolling landscape of the Transylvanian plateau. Huedin had a market, I realised, as I ran into a milling stream of horses and carts: many carried chickens or pigs in rough wooden crates, and passengers, crammed beside the driver or overflowing on to the crates in the back; often a spare horse, calf or buffalo followed on a rope behind. A couple of fields on the outskirts of the town seethed with people from all the villages in the district, Romanians, Hungarians, gipsies. The crowd made a raucous sea where men shouted and pigs squealed, and people were tossed this way and that as a horse started suddenly or a yelling driver tried to force a way through.

Gipsy women strutted among the sombre peasants in loud, fiery-coloured bands, lithe girls or haggard mothers perpetually pregnant or breast-feeding. Their men dominated the horse market. The narrow waggons in that section were filled with children; in one, beneath a hooped cover that was patched together from polythene sheeting and bright fabrics, three small girls slept entwined, half-naked: like cherubs until they woke and turned on me begging brown eyes.

I bought lunch in the town. But Huedin seemed not a country town so much as a strip of high-rise suburb with no city attached. The single restaurant had run out of food and the shelves of the bakery were bare, so I waited twenty minutes in a cafeteria for a small boiled sausage, a gherkin and a hundred-gram chunk of grey bread. No-one in the queue, not even the three gipsy women behind me, spoke. It was as if everyone was listening to the hum of the refrigerator or watching the flicker of the single fluorescent strip over the counter.

I was glad to escape over grassy sweeps of land to Cluj.

*   *   *

Cluj lay at the centre of a huge building site like an old city under siege. I came in through a labyrinth of streets that had been torn and ridged by heavy vehicles, over muddy tracks where the road dissolved before an unbuilt bridge, past white skeletons of high-rise flats.

German Klausenburg, Hungarian Koloszvár, is the historic capital of Transylvania and the centre of Hungarian culture there, though its present official name of Cluj-Napoca appends the name of the Dacian town which once stood on the site and so calls attention to the Romanian right to the territory. At its heart it is still Kolosvár, in its dignified public buildings and rambling university, and the white-and-ochre opera house with bronze chariots rearing from twin towers. My hotel was the banana-coloured Continental, decorated with pretty white pilasters and frothy sweeps of acanthus leaves. Either this or the turreted Hotel Metropol across the square must formerly have been the New York where Patrick Leigh Fermor had drunk cocktails fifty years earlier on his journey to Istanbul. In those days the barman at the New York was famed across Central Europe for his original concoctions. In those days a traveller could walk all the way to Istanbul and make the walk a way of life without travel and visa restrictions or the necessity to exchange ten US dollars in advance at the border for each day he meant to spend in the country.

Yet Cluj seemed still an attractive place. A Gothic church filled the heart of the square; its roof was in course of restoration, by volunteers apparently, as a gang of young people worked through the early evening unloading and sorting a batch of new red tiles, passing them from hand to hand along a chain. They worked easily, talking and laughing. In the rose garden before the church the lazy and old dreamed on park benches. There was a café close by where tables were set outside beneath a striped yellow awning.

I must still have been thinking of cocktails. When I went in to buy a drink I did not expect the bar to be so crude. A few older peasant women sat among the beer-drinking men, but no young women. As I elbowed through the crowd with my beer, a drunk seated at a table leered up at me and put a hand between my legs. A farce ensued. In reflex, I threw my glass of beer over him, and found myself punched on the jaw in return. I fell to the floor, as much from shock as from the force of the blow, then struggled up among the tables at the centre of a clearing of drinkers like a felled cowboy in a saloon. It made me angrier still that not a hand was put out to help me. I launched then into what must have been an absurd display of outraged Britishness, demanding the *policia, militia, polis, poliẓei*, POLICE, in any and every language that came to mind.

I guess they must have got the message but no one did a thing. It was I who spotted a tall blue-uniformed policeman across the square and dragged him over. My temper had not yet cooled enough for me to think quite what action I expected him to take: something to do with a stubby pencil and a notebook, the taking of names and of the statements of witnesses.

But I and my attacker were hustled swiftly out of the sun, down a corridor and into the windowless cloakroom, a white cell filled with rails of bare coat-hangers. There, after a brief volley of words, the policeman started to give the drunk a moderate beating-up. I got the feeling that crueller blows could have been delivered if necessary – and would be on occasion. There was a brief pause only as he turned and slugged the man's drinking companion who had attempted to intervene; this second drinker was dealt with more effectively by a new arrival, a little rat-like man who smoothly handled him out and slammed the door.

He then turned to me. 'I spik English,' he said unconvincingly. He had shifty brown eyes, slicked-back hair and a pencil moustache; he wore an aggressively tailored grey suit, no raincoat since it was not yet September. He was the archetypal secret policeman.

He produced a phrasebook and read out something that sounded more like German.

'*Nu e Engleẓă,*' I said. '*E Germană.*'

'*Ba e Engleẓă.*'

'*Nu. Cred e Germană.*' I put out my hand for the book. Reluctantly, as if it were confidential information, he passed it to me. It was the polyglot phrasebook issued to Romanian police, containing sections in Russian, French, German and English. I turned to the English section as indicated in the contents list: it was German. I tried the page where the German was indexed: English. God help any German or English tourist who got arrested here. There were dialogues concerning thefts and driving offences but nothing specifically applicable to this situation.

Meantime he had fallen into discussion with the uniformed policeman. The only word I could make out clearly, repeated a couple of times, was '*biciclista*'. (This was curious since I had arrived in the town a couple of hours earlier and had taken my bicycle straight into the hotel; I did not think I looked obviously a cyclist.) By now my attacker was weeping and cowering among the coat-hangers; whenever he moved forward he got a casual slap in the face.

The secret policeman decided to improvise. 'Where is . . . husband?'

'What's that got to do with it?'

They consulted again. I was relieved when the waiter knocked on the door and introduced a young man who taught English at the university. He was apologetic, 'I am sorry, in our country it is not customary for a woman to travel unprotected.'

'So what are they going to do?'

As I spoke the big policeman threw a few more swipes at the culprit, so sloppily that I was caught on the nose as the teacher tried to pull me back out of range.

'There's no point in this,' I said. 'Can't we all get out of here?'

'Yes,' said the teacher. 'That's the best idea.' And spoke in Romanian. My attacker now came forward and gave my hand a servile kiss. The policeman sneered.

We emerged on to the square. 'That was disgusting. Brutal!' I said.

'But this is Romania,' the teacher answered calmly.

I wish I had stayed to talk to him. I was sorry that he had been dragged into such an unpleasant scene. But at that moment I wanted only to escape. I went back to the hotel and ordered a beer on room service. It came a half hour or so later.

What was it the Englishman in Budapest had said? Like cycling through the fourteenth century. I woke in the morning and saw the bruise on my face, and thought of the savage outbursts that marked the century of the Black Death. I was not sure I liked the comparison.

Breakfast was in the 'Brasserie' downstairs, a long room with a high barrelled ceiling curling with neo-baroque plasterwork. There should have been coffee from the expresso machine behind the steel-topped bar but there wasn't. Stout middle-aged men in brown suits sat uncomfortably on low stools and smoked. A bluish cloud hung above them, soaking up the sunlight that came through the tall windows. This, at least, was the twentieth century, but it felt more like Mussolini's Italy than the 1980s. The impression gathered all morning. It had something to do with the cream-coloured lace curtains and metal chandelier in my room, the tobacco colours of the stairs, the heavy upholstered sofa on the landing and the hard-faced woman who was sitting there when I came down. She had on a straight maroon skirt, dark stockings, high heels; the Romanian taste seemed to be for dark colours, like those of the glassware in shop windows: plum, indigo, topaz.

The clothes of people on the streets were generally sombre; men often had double-breasted jackets, and women too wore tailored suits. The styles harked back to before the war. (Later a Romanian I knew in London pointed out that most of the clothes were probably hand-me-downs; it is always the heavy, tailored things that last longest.) It is said that the Romanians resemble the Italians, but they had a weight that seemed quite un-Italian, that was perhaps caught from the Slavs. Not just that many were short and squat, but that their faces were generally impassive, that animation seemed to break out like violence: crude and unpredictable. They pushed down the streets with a fixed look on their faces; behind it lay the brooding pressure of poverty and the crowding of the city, the influx of Romanians from other provinces, as well as from the countryside, to the half-built new developments. On the skyline above the flats cranes stood idle on a Tuesday morning as if some great docks were on strike.

Shopping was long toil. I had heard that those who wanted things were at the shops at four, five, six o'clock in the morning and that the shelves were quickly bare. By the time I went out there were long queues outside the few shops that still had some meat, fruit or vegetables – though the latter were best bought at the market where peasants brought the produce from their private plots. I was lucky: I had bought fruit and tomatoes from people in the villages. But I waited twenty minutes or more for bread. The queue was stationary most of that time while the van from the bakery was unloaded; there were already some loaves on the shelves but no-one saw fit to serve the customers until the van had driven off. The first woman to the front of the queue was stopped as she left the shop; those behind reached out their hands to feel the loaves. Were they fresh? No. The message soon passed down the line and a few gave up, to save their ration for a new loaf. Why the bread was already stale on delivery I could not imagine.

The extreme food shortages were in large part due to the austerity measures invoked by Ceauşescu since the early 1980s, with the proud stated intention of paying off Romania's entire ten billion dollar foreign debt to the West by 1990, and with an utter disregard for people's basic needs. Bread and meat had been rationed: a woman told me she had four hundred grams of bread a day and one kilo of meat for three months. Milk and dairy products were almost impossible to find and seemed to be on sale exclusively on the black market; once in a hotel I met a peasant boy shuffling down the corridor, a Murillo shepherd in sheepskin waistcoat and conical felt cap, who drew me aside and showed me what he had in the woven bag on his shoulder as if it were diamonds: a goat's cheese wrapped in muslin.

The irony, as people said, was that the enormous sums of money borrowed in the first place had been thrown away on disastrous and overblown industrial developments, such as a metallurgical industry for which Romania cannot supply the raw materials, and a massive oil-refining capacity, far above internal requirements, which was hit hard by the oil crisis of the 1970s. The current blanket restrictions on use of power and fuel served only to make the existing industry ever less productive – the more so as economies on maintenance reduced the efficiency of ageing plants. Romania's gigantic leap forward, years too late, on the Stalinist road of heavy industry, had become a slide backwards towards underdevelopment.

Constantly people would say to me: 'It was not so bad last year'; 'If you had been here a year ago you would have thought it was better – two years, three years ago things were not nearly so hard'; or 'If only you had come ten years ago . . .'

The streets around the university were almost empty since it was still the summer holiday. I took refuge among the faded neo-classical buildings and courtyards shrouded in creepers. At the end of a broad street I came to the little fifteenth-century evangelical church. Inside, the arms of great Transylvanian families were painted on the backs of the choir stalls, still rich with heraldic colour. It was light, Gothic, calm. The people who trickled in for the evening service belonged to a different Cluj, to Klausenburg. The first to arrive were an elderly couple. The woman, neat and grey, tapped her hat crisply when she saw me and went on to her pew; her husband lagged behind, a long, stooped man in a loose summer suit, panama and malacca cane in hand. He nodded to me with an antiquated courtesy, drooping further his dark oval face, blinking his eyes slowly in their sallow hollows.

'Good evening.' He spoke in German, with a long pause between each phrase. 'So nice . . . to see a new face. Where . . . have you come from?'

'From England.'

'Ah ... English.' He sighed and his sigh conjured up the western fringe of Europe. 'So, what do you think of Romania?'

I said that the landscape was very beautiful but that it did not look a very easy place to live.

'You are right there ...' he answered. 'Take care.'

I was anxious to leave Cluj. The incident in the bar had made me jumpy. And I distrusted the staff in the hotel. There were two youngish men at reception and an older woman. The woman was clearly in charge, stern, abrupt, chain-smoking. She was a big, square woman, incongruously youthful in her dress: her black hair was scraped back into a pony tail, her eyes were ringed in mauve, and she wore a denim jacket patterned with silver studs. When they asked me questions, as they did all too frequently, I thought it best to be generous with information – though my plans were in truth no more a collection of vague notions. I had a sensation that they already knew where the *biciclista* was headed: the news that I was going to Istanbul was received with the boredom that accompanies a confirmation of established fact. It was the woman who gave me the bill when I left on the second morning. She asked what road I was taking. I said I had decided to go north, to Maramureş. I repeated what a friend had once told me, that Maramureş was the most beautiful place in all of Europe and that its folk culture was quite unique. ('And while you're there, pay an exalted respect to Romanian culture,' he had added, 'that'll go down well.')

'It is our richness,' she answered creamily.

'But also your secret, I think, since I see no other foreign tourists here.' I couldn't resist it.

'Not at all. We have many foreign visitors here, many English people like yourself.' She looked out into the empty foyer as if it were buzzing with coach tours.

9

All morning a grey haze obscured the hills. There was only the road, and the railway tracks that ran alongside, and people walking in the dust of the verge: men with plastic briefcases, satchels, sacks. A gipsy family was on the move, two men in front bent beneath white sacks. The women were flashes of colour. In the opacity they were rootless; they could have been two thousand miles to the east.

The towns of Gherla and Dej loomed drearily. They were fringed with building sites and smoking factories with heaps of metal outside like exposed bones. Even at the centre the towns were held in transition, half crumbling, half new with a uniform grey modernity. The main square in Gherla was still dominated by the massive baroque church built by Armenian settlers; its walls were a fungal green and its great doors were padlocked.

On the edges of the towns and in the big villages were co-operative farmyards: machine stations with ranks of trucks, tractors and combines – half of them rusting and stripped of tyres – and huge barns. In the wide fields of the plain around Cluj and here on the flat land of the Someş valley, collective farming was evident, though the land in the hills was still divided into peasant smallholdings. I assumed that it was the collectives which placed the slogans along the road in each village: CEAUŞESCU EROISM or EPOCA CEAUŞESCU, EPOCA GLORIOASA. Soldiers had been drafted in to help with the harvest; their uniforms were dark olive dabs in the lines of pickers in the paprika fields. It looked slow, back-breaking work, inching down the rows to pick the reddening fruits from plants only a couple of feet high.

In Baia Mare I had introductions to two people. The first I managed to contact was Dinu, a local journalist, and we met at the Hotel Carpati,

78

on a terrace of cracked concrete overlooking the litter-strewn river bed.

Dinu wore a tawny tweed jacket that was thin at the elbows. He seemed mild, brown and philosophical, a Romanian from Transylvania, now in his mid-forties with a couple of children at school. He was charming but impenetrable. He spoke a smooth French that was far better than mine yet he was halted sometimes by questions I asked as if I had used words that he didn't know. I suspected this was an habitual caution, a play for time to choose the most suitable answer. Discretion must be second nature for a journalist in such a country. I had glanced at Romanian newspapers; it was easy, if you had a smattering of Latin languages, to get the gist of the articles if not to read them. The text concentrated on a detailed record of presidential speeches and official visits. The President and his wife were pictured on almost every page, the same small, stiff figures reappearing on new podia, receiving new bouquets, against different factory, laboratory and institutional backdrops. I wondered what Dinu did all day.

He was a reporter for one of the national newspapers, covering a wide area of northern Transylvania from Baia Mare to the Hungarian border and east to the passes into Moldavia. He travelled a lot, visited factories. And whenever he could he went to see the churches. He seemed to know every one in his area and volunteered a rambling but enthusiastic lecture on the wooden buildings of the Maramureş district, telling me which were his favourites and which I should on no account miss.

As he talked he tinkered with an unlit cigarette, waiting for a glass of wine to smoke it with. He seemed faintly nervous, kept on talking about the churches, wouldn't let the conversation die. When at last the wine came, a shuffle through the pockets of his jacket produced no matches. He rose with an almost Japanese bow, and got a light at the next table.

I took the chance to ask about the villages. Did he know about the recent furore in the British press?

'All propaganda,' he said lightly. 'How could anyone destroy and rebuild so many villages in an instant? It's a physical impossibility.'

'But President Ceauşescu has said that of the country's thirteen thousand villages, seven thousand will be "systemised" by the year 2000. Or that's what the papers say he said.'

Dinu nodded.

'And "systemised" means demolished and relocated, doesn't it?'

'Yes and no. You see, it's only a slogan. Look at those round numbers. It's obvious. And you people decide to take it literally.'

'Who does?'

'The West. No, the Hungarians. They use it for propaganda. Everyone knows they would invade Transylvania again, given the chance. Saving the villages would be only a pretext. And the Western Europeans believe everything the Hungarians tell them! How many British journalists come to Romania?'

Few Western journalists were granted visas to come and see for themselves. I asked what he thought the slogan meant.

He explained the systemisation policy as almost a natural evolution. In the course of industrialisation many young people had moved to the towns, and life was hard for those who remained in the scattered villages. Also primitive: had I seen the hovels where some of the peasants lived? In time, such places would disappear. It sounded very reasonable.

'But if seven thousand villages are condemned . . .'

'Condemned? No, no.' He corrected me with the air of a librarian smoothing down a ruffled page. 'Just that some villages will go.'

'Well, some of these villages must be in this district?'

'Oh, I wouldn't think so. Around Baia Mare the villages are prosperous. Many people have jobs in the town but also have a piece of land of their own in a village. They can grow a little food there, for themselves or to sell; and the wives will also do some work at home, embroidery or weaving. So then they can build new houses, good and solid. You must have seen some on your way from Cluj.'

I had seen a few, unmistakably middle-class in style, with ostentatious carved gateways that crammed together what I suspected were bogus folk motifs, somehow lacking the individuality of the gateways of traditional cottages. What of the villages in the more mountainous parts of Maramureş?

'Change is coming even there. There are some new houses. Though the young people are going to the cities.'

'Then they will be gradually depopulated?'

'No. In regional centres such as Sighetu Marmaţiei industry is being expanded. Many country people will be able to find work there. And the villages themselves have strong foundations, with traditional cottage industries, weaving, handicrafts. No, those villages will stay.'

I tried a few other areas, but every one seemed to have something going for it. The seven thousand were always somewhere else.

*   *   *

I had arranged to meet Sándor the next day outside a café in a little square in the old Hungarian part of town.

He was late, came running at six. 'I am sorry, I came straight from the factory. There is some crazy production plan so now we never finish work. And I could not change. Please forgive my work clothes. Is the coffee real?'

It wasn't. But they had stopped serving coffee anyway; he came back from the counter with two bowls of sage-green ice-cream. 'Have you tried Romanian ice-cream?'

I had seen it, always the same colour. It was more ice than cream but cool on the tongue. 'What flavour is it?'

'Who knows?' he said. 'Green.'

Sándor was a big man, too big for the flimsy table beneath the plane trees. He was an engineer in one of Baia Mare's metallurgical plants. His sleeves were rolled up over muscular brown arms and his broad hands were engrained with dirt. But beneath the industrial grime he had an air of the mountains. His family came from one of the towns in Harghita, Hungarians in the most Hungarian province of Transylvania, on the easternmost curve of the Carpathians. He had straight Magyar features, green eyes, hair that glinted gold against brown.

When he was a child he was always running off to the mountains. When he was twelve, he walked for a week and spoke to no-one. And now he went up there whenever he had the chance. He knew a cave where you could camp and never be found. In the forest there were mushrooms and herbs from which you could make tea; some were medicinal. If they didn't have to make this damn production quota he would show me. 'Do not waste your time in the towns here; they are nothing now. Go to the mountains. That is Transylvania.'

He walked to the flat where his girlfriend lived, a couple of sparsely furnished rooms in a newish block. Erica was Hungarian too but looked Saxon: blonde, big-boned and strong, stronger in a way than Sándor, for she had stillness in place of his ebullience. Her five-year-old son was as fair as she but scampering and monkeyish. He was sent off to bed in the next room and we sat and drank our way through a small bottle of brandy I had managed to buy for hard currency at the hotel. It was Romanian and harsh, but brandy, and impossible to get for Romanian *lei*.

Erica listened mainly as Sándor talked, but once interrupted to ask what English people knew of Transylvania. I said that those who read the papers knew now about the villages, but that to many the news seemed strange since they had not been sure until then that Transylvania was real.

She winced at this. 'Because of the Dracula story?'

'Yes. But tell me, are the stories about the villages real?'

'Oh yes, I think so. Everyone thinks so, though they may say otherwise.' Her voice was hard. 'And what do Americans know about us?'

'Probably less since they're further away. Most people have seen a Dracula movie. But I've met Americans in the Midwest who didn't seem to know where England was, asked which American state London was in.'

Sándor asked if I had heard bluegrass music in America. 'One day I will go to Kentucky. To the Appalachians. Or to Vermont. Could I find something there like my mountains?'

'Almost,' I said. I had not seen the Appalachians but I had stayed once in a cabin in Vermont, by a waterfall in a forest. A friend was building it for himself but had not finished, and you woke up in the morning and went out to wash and saw deer by the pool at the base of the waterfall. I was there in October when the birch trees were bare and their white trunks and branches were like the skeins of a net thrown over the brown mountainsides. High up there were fewer trees and you could still pick blueberries among the lichen-covered rocks. I told them Vermont was beautiful but the mountains did not stretch out like the Carpathians: there was not the rolling pasture. Nor the haystacks that made patterns across it. Nor the peasants or the history.

'Maybe we could do without.' Sándor said how the peasants made him sad. 'They see only the ground at their feet and the sky right above them. They are like a weight on this country. Some people say that a peasant makes the ideal worker. He comes to the city, freed at last from the land; he goes into the factory but he takes with him the mentality of the land. He accepts bad conditions, pay cuts, stupid orders, impossible quotas, as if they were rain or drought. Like they came from heaven. Maybe that's why people are so fatalistic in Romania: even the workers are still peasants in their hearts. At the end of the war, more than three-quarters of the population were on the land. Now it is less than thirty per cent. Minds do not change so fast.'

Sándor's father was an engineer, as his father also had been. He had never thought of doing anything else, and the job was comparatively well paid and high status. But every day he hated it because he saw such waste: the waste of men's sweat, of resources, of money the country did not have. They earned less than they had a couple of years before, and worked longer hours, even Sundays. Their factory was famous yet it produced nothing that was either useful or saleable. It was there and they worked there simply because it was prestigious, because it made someone look grand: 'That's not Socialism.'

'No,' I said, 'it's tyranny.'

'It was you who said that!'

As we walked back across the dark town, Sándor told me about himself and Erica. It was just temporary, he said. Her husband, the boy's father, was in Germany and she expected to be able to leave soon. Sándor was sad; he said he loved her calm. He thought she loved him but if she could go, she must, for herself and for the child. How could he ask her to get a divorce – and stay? But until she left he would look after her. Since her husband had gone, almost two years ago, she had had problems at her work and now she had had no work at all for seven or eight months; he gave her money and food parcels sometimes came through from Germany.

I asked if he would leave.

That was not possible. When he was twenty, he had been engaged to a German girl. They had lived one summer wild in the mountains. Then she went with her family to Germany, and he put in his papers: if you were leaving to marry or to join a spouse two years was the usual delay. But after a year she had jilted him. I did not at first see the full significance of this. Sándor explained that the relationship was one thing: he could forgive her for changing her mind; she was only nineteen. But how could she take away from him the possibility of leaving the country? That was twelve years ago and still the authorities held it against him. Recently he had applied for a job in Russia; he was well qualified for it but they had refused to give him a passport. He had got angry, demanded why.

'And did they tell you?'

'In the end. They called it "lack of moral trust".'

'What does that mean?'

He shrugged.

The phone rang in my room at the hotel early next morning. Dinu had come to say goodbye. While waiting downstairs he had brought life to the blubbery face of the girl stranded behind the 'Tourism' desk, who now wobbled her features into a smile and handed me detailed maps of the Maramureş district. These had, to all appearances, not existed when I had asked for them the day before. Dinu had also taken it upon himself to book me a hotel in Sighetu Marmaţiei for the next two nights – two because he recommended a detour to the famous 'Happy Cemetery' at Săpînţa where every grave bore a joke on it and I would witness the uniquely humorous Romanian approach to death. (Sándor had hinted that I might give this a miss, complaining how this particular piece of folk culture had been bureaucratised and commercialised.) Over breakfast Dinu once again schooled me on the churches I should visit, marking each one on the map and which road I should take. I began to wonder unkindly where the line was drawn between hospitality and control. I thought I would steal a day, ignore Săpînţa and go on ahead.

The church at Surdeşti had a spire like an arrow. It was all I could see at first above the trees. The shingled point tapered upwards from the square shaft of the belfry, and four dwarf spires stood sentry at its base, mimicking exactly its proportion and the little flourish of the eaves. It was like the spires of the Gothic churches of the Nyírség. As there, I looked for storks skimming overhead. But the storks had already left for Africa.

A cart track ran the short distance down to the church from the hilltop. It ended beside a house that had a steep overhanging roof and broad-planked walls, like a Japanese farmhouse, and vines trailing wild and unpruned over its porch. A wattle fence enclosed the churchyard, with an arched gateway and close by a water barrel, full and gleaming at the brim. The vine leaves were translucent, silky green in contrast to the various coarse darknesses of wattle and planks and shingles.

Walnut trees, some of them already with yellow leaves, surrounded the church, and gravestones waist-high in grass. A scythed path led to the porch, which was galleried like the porches of the village houses, with carved posts and a low carved fence in front that supported a lectern for outdoor services. The walls of the church were low, barely a person's height, squat beneath the broad eaves and steep-pitched shingle roof. They were made of massive planks, each the full length of the nave, slotted into huge rough joints. The apse was narrower and gently curved like the stern of a ship. Halfway up the walls, all round the church, ran a carved rail like a three-inch cable. So far inland, the church might have been built by the carpenters of the ark.

Above the cable a few tiny windows were cut at random into the walls, and memorial crosses were nailed on, some finely carved, some blunt and plain. The weathering of the wood showed which were the newest crosses, still reddish against the predominant dark grey-brown, and pale outlines revealed where older crosses had fallen away. A few of the planks also were reddish and new, and there were patches of lighter-coloured shingles where sections of roof had been mended.

A tall boy came through the walnuts. He had seen my bike at the gate and brought the key. Through the door, the church became Byzantine. It was divided into narthex, nave, and apse behind a carved iconostasis, each room progressively more dim and dense beneath the hull-like roof, covered in paintings that had been clouded by centuries of candlesmoke. The boy pointed out the different subjects on the walls: the stiff figures of saints and martyrs in the narthex, and over the entrance a cosmological drawing of sun and moon enclosed in a circle; in the nave, Jacob's ladder, Moses with the tablets of the law, the evangelists, Elijah in his chariot drawn by winged horses, an angel of the Apocalypse with a face like the sun, and the beast with seven heads rising from the sea. They were peasant paintings, with naive faces and crooked perspectives, and the two rooms were decorated like a peasant house with embroidered cloths draped above the windows and doorways, above individual icons and above each section of the iconostasis. A bare bulb dangled on a cord beside the unused brass chandelier.

He had practised a spiel in schoolboy French. The church, he said, was eighteenth-century and the finest in the district, with the tallest spire, fifty-five metres high. His mother was the official caretaker; they lived in the house by the gate. He liked to show people round but there weren't so many foreigners nowadays. When I asked what sort of wood the church was built from he thought awhile, then admitted that he didn't know the word in French. But he could show me a tree. We went across the grassy cemetery and into a field to where a young oak was growing.

Beyond Surdeşti, a pass led through to the wide depression of the Maramureş country. Rivers run down into this basin from the Carpathian watersheds to the north, east and south, to meet with the Tisza, which forms the border here between Romania and Russia. In the past Maramureş has been isolated by its geography. Only very recently have roads made even the major valleys easily accessible, and walking is still a common way to get around. Béla Bartók walked through the region early this century in search of folk music; he believed that the songs he heard in the hills, almost oriental in their style, derived directly from those of pre-Christian times.

It was the last day of August. The pass climbed through substantial hills rather than mountains, great rolls of land beneath tall beech forests. The descent was gentler than the climb, with long views out over the beeches, whose leaves were just dulled with bronze tarnish.

I had lunch lying on an island of grass in a mountain stream: stale grey bread with some of the salami from Debrecen, and a couple of crisp apples pilfered from trees along the road. The high bank hid me from the meadow above, into which two girls brought their livestock to graze. Lazily I listened as they chattered and sang in breathy voices, and at last, with a wakening splash of water from the stream, I got up to take a look at them. I crossed the stream and climbed the bank. They must have been only ten or so, girls with long plaits and cotton skirts and kerchiefs in scarlet and green. The two of them were practising a dance, each taking a couple of skips then turning and twizzling round to set their plaits and full skirts flying. The herd, a couple of buffaloes and three cows, chomped on regardless around their feet.

'*Bună ziua*,' I called, and they stopped mid-whirl to gaze dizzily at me. One hung back with the buffalo but curiosity got the better of the other. She came forward on long legs like a deer, a little girl with astonishingly golden hair and green eyes. I was sorry I did not have much left over from my lunch to share with them.

The Iza valley runs south-east from Sighetu Marmaţiei. At this season the river was low, threading mildly among rocks. At the sides of the valley, eccentric hills started up to the high ranges. They were scattered with woods and pastures, cut up by rectangles of maize and stubble; sometimes the jagged points of trees ruffled their tops or their slopes were rippled by the outlines of abandoned terracing.

In the fields at the heart of the valley people were making hay. I rested with my back to a tree and watched the women in wide skirts as they bent down and swept the hay into rows with their long rakes, or went down the rows and turned the hay to dry it more. Others, with a twist of the rake, raised bundles of hay on to new stacks that were skewered about a central pole, or draped them across horizontal drying racks. Each movement flowed into the next, the sweeping to the turning to the raising, the rounded figures working in time. At the edge of the field stood their waggon, and the horse grazing.

Other women came to wash clothes in the broad river bed. The rhythmic smack as they beat them against flat rocks carried up to the road. To me, it sounded of India; if I closed my eyes I could picture the long coloured lengths of saris spread to dry on ghats and riverbanks. But this was Europe. The women here were pale northerners.

When I came into the next village, a crooked figure laboured up the road towards me pushing a barrow. An old woman, face cross-hatched with age. She wore no boots but hobbled in felt leggings tied with thongs. A barefoot child helped her, a fair-skinned girl with Baltic blue eyes and pale blonde plaits. Suddenly I realised what struck me so about these people. The girl seemed a child of some extinct European race. An anachronism. A medieval child in a green landscape, beneath a tree thick with reddening apples, yet her face was so familiar. It was only a small distance that separated us.

Outside the gateways of their houses, women sat spinning black and white wool, their daughters and grand-daughters seated beside them. A white-haired man in loose white shirt and trousers, with a sheepskin coat slung over one shoulder, drove an empty waggon by; a hay cart followed slowly, the thin horse straining to drag up a slight incline a load so high that it brushed against the overhanging trees and left wisps of hay in their branches.

I walked down a rough track through the village to the forge beside the river. There was a flash of fire within, a red shower of sparks. A woman in black worked the foot-bellows, and the blacksmith looked up and saw me and called for American cigarettes. In a pool of sunlight by the bright-leaved willows an old man in white homespun and conical felt hat stood and stared dottily at me. A gang of ragged children began to trail behind, demanding gum, bonbons, biros, money. The people and the images crowded in on me and I felt a creeping tension I had known before only in the face of the acknowledged third world: some combination of pity, anger, fear, guilt, and the urge to escape. Black pigs snuffled in the deep drains alongside the road, and in the fenced yards before those too-picturesque wooden houses. The split logs piled on their porches, the strings of onions and drying chillies, the piled hay in the barns, spoke of the squirrel labour of preparation for winter. I wondered how it was then, when the tracks and squalid farmyards turned to icy mud.

The village was called Ieud. It was long and sprawling and had two churches, the older of which was built in the fourteenth century. Like other churches in the villages of the valley, this one stood on a small hill, and its cemetery, crowded with wooden crosses and the haphazard hummocks of graves, was planted with old plum trees. Fruit and ancient silvered branches had been cast to the ground in recent storms – the same late-summer storms as I had experienced in Hungary: the Nyírség was only a hundred miles off here, though I had had to come much further. In this church, as in those of the Nyírség, the scent of battered plums hung like incense. Yet in place of the white Calvinism of Hungary was a dense mysticism. In the dark, behind the iconostasis, in the apocalyptic paintings on the walls, lay a sense of a remote and fateful God. A medieval God. I felt the passive weight of centuries on the place.

The valley was eerie. I went to look at the church in another village I passed and happened to read the painted lettering on one of the new metal crosses in the graveyard: a name and the dates August 1924–December 1988. But that day was the first of September 1988. At least the name wasn't mine.

10

EPOCA LUMINOASA: EPOCA CEAUŞESCU.

Towards nightfall I came to the mining town of Borşa, a grey settlement straggling along a pot-holed street. The hills that closed in on either side had already taken away the light. There was a hotel set back from the road, a ramshackle concrete hotel with a weather-stained sign. I had left it too late to find a place to camp.

The receptionist was a pink-cheeked country girl who looked constrained by her tailored clothes. When I asked for a room she set to a glum study of the register though a key hung spare in every dusty pigeonhole behind the desk.

'*Poloneză?*'

'*Nu.*'

'*Socialistă?*' I gave her my passport. 'English!' A dark man who had been lounging in a chair across the hall came and looked at the passport over her shoulder. He nodded to her as he went back round the desk. 'Yes,' she said, 'we have a room.'

'How much?'

'A thousand *lei.*'

That was more than £80 at the official exchange rate. You might have thought it was the hotel at the end of the world.

'For one person only, eight hundred *lei.* That is with foreigners' tax. Because you are English.'

'If I came from somewhere else, would it be less?'

'Perhaps. For French, Italians, it is the same. But less for citizens of Socialist countries, Soviet Union, Bulgaria, Poland, Czechoslovakia, DDR, etcetera.'

'Ah.' I wondered how far this distinction went. 'How about Chinese?'

'Chinese? Then I make a telephone call. We have never had a Chinese here.' She looked to the dark man for help but he scowled and went out. Once we were alone she relaxed a little, leaned over the desk and asked if I had anything from my country. A packet of Kent cigarettes won me a substantial tax exemption, and a suite on the top floor with a sitting room and plastic flowers in a glass vase.

In the dingy restaurant a table was laid for me, with half a paper napkin, neatly torn, folded beside the fork. (Were even napkins rationed here?) I was the only customer who had anything to eat; at three distant tables three lone men were getting silently and staggeringly drunk. Lucky they weren't staying at the hotel: they would never have made it upstairs. The carpet fell sheer and loose down each concrete flight and you had to grope cautiously through it, in the inevitable near-darkness, for every step. Dogs in the town howled all through the night.

I left early and climbed through silent pinewoods. There were shepherds on the high pasture. Over a pass the road ran down into Moldavia along the course of the Bistriţa river. In places the ravine opened out a little, and a few fields were set beside a lone house on the valley floor. And at one point where the forest came down steep on both sides three men walked ahead of me carrying scythes that glinted on their shoulders. They turned off the road there, into the trees, up a track that must have led to some hidden field or settlement.

Moldavia was one of the three medieval Romanian principalities. In 1600 it was first united with Wallachia and Transylvania to form Romania. Only for a year. Apart from that it had a history distinct from the others, with its own princes and wars, until the pan-Romanian dream – and the requirements of international politics – reunited it with Wallachia in the mid-nineteenth century, then with Transylvania after the first world war for a second brief interlude. In 1940 the Russians seized the northern and easternmost sectors of the province to form a separate Soviet Republic.

It was around the middle of the fourteenth century that a prince of Maramureş, Bogdan, tired of Hungarian domination and crossed the Carpathians to found an independent state in the area around the river Moldova, where already there were some Romanian settlements. A more picturesque tale, one of the many on the subject, says that he went over the mountains to hunt the European bison, that great animal of the Russian and Polish plains, which never strayed west of the Carpathians. He took with him his favourite hunting dog, Molda, whose name he gave to the lush new territory he found.

There are more myths and fewer facts known about Romanian history than about that of any other country in Europe. Light comes earlier to Transylvania, light cast from the west, as its history becomes bound up with that of Hungary. The lands beyond remain in shadow. During the eleventh, twelfth and thirteenth centuries, when the Hungarian kings were consolidating their power, sending Saxons and Szeklers to found towns on the fringes of Transylvania, northern Moldavia was still prey to the Mongol and Cuman tribes who roamed in from the steppes. Almost throughout their history, Moldavia and Wallachia have had to face east, with the mountains at their backs. (From this direction also come the prevailing winds, from east and also north and south-east, from Russia and the Black Sea, while west winds sweep across Hungary into Transylvania.)

From the east came the Mongols, and after them the Turks. At the fall of Constantinople in 1453, the Turks already held all of the Balkan peninsula south of the Danube, apart from a pocket of resistance in the Albanian mountains. Wallachia had acknowledged Ottoman suzerainty. Muscovy still fought off the Mongols. Moldavia stood alone in the Orthodox world – and got little more support from western Christianity than Constantinople had before it. Yet strangely enough it produced a heroic Christian champion, a generation or so too late for the Crusades. Stephen the Great was pious and cruel and medieval; he routed the Turks a couple of times in repeated campaigns, only to recognise that Moldavia was bound to lose in the end: it is said that his deathbed advice to his son was to submit to the Turks if honourable terms could be found – or to die fighting. So, in the sixteenth century Moldavia too fell under Ottoman rule, though both Romanian states retained greater autonomy than that of the Turkish pashalics south of the Danube.

Scattered across northern Moldavia are churches and monasteries founded by Stephen and by later princes and boyars. Their style reflects the oddity of the country's position, cut off from the Balkan metropolitans to the south and from Kiev across the plains to the north. Their Byzantine painted walls are pierced by Gothic windows: to the provincial workmen who built the churches, ideas came as easily over the mountains from Gothic Transylvania as from any Byzantine source.

Often, the paintings cover exterior as well as interior walls: apostles, saints, seraphim with enfolded wings, Bible stories played out against stylised desert landscapes and Byzantine cities that local painters must have dreamt up from the evidence of icons. One series tells a comic-strip story of an earlier siege of Constantinople, updated with artistic licence to show medieval Moldavians, rustics in tight hose and liripipe hats, fighting turbanned Ottomans who wield crescent swords in their hands. And almost every church has a Last Judgement, with Turks – and sometimes Jews – tumbling, burning and drowning in the river of fire, while the chosen climb a ladder to a heaven that gleams gold with the haloes of the saints. The colours are generally only a little faded, the greens a little gone to blue, but lapis, gold and red ochre stand out strong after four centuries – except on the walls that face into the northern winds: there the weather has washed away all but phantom outlines.

The churches are long and narrow, the curve of the apse exaggerated by the broad overhang of the roof; they sit curled in on themselves like cats in the landscape. The deep roof gives way to a slim hexagonal tower in place of either Gothic spire or Byzantine dome; yet from the inside it appears more like a dome, rising on a double series of pendentives placed star-like one above the other. The heart of the church seems purely Byzantine. Gothic windows do not penetrate into the inner rooms where the congregation crowd close for services. The paintings on these walls are dark, their surfaces black and waxy from centuries of candlesmoke.

Yet it struck me that there was another element at play besides the Byzantine. Was there not something Slav in the illumination, and in the gravity with which the deep roofs seemed to root the churches to the earth? It hinted of Russia rather than the Byzantine south. And how much stronger that impression must be in winter, when snow drifts against the northern walls.

Since the nation was formed, Romanians have emphasised their Latin roots, so evident in the language and in the very name of the country. Yet it seems too convenient a simplification to trace descent purely from the Dacians and Romans: as if by so doing Romania freed itself not only of the political domination of first Turks and then Russians, but also of some heavy, Eastern European, Slav fate. Another influence seems apparent at times, deep-rooted beside the Latin culture though it may be ignored like a garden weed. Romanians have so identified themselves with Latinised Western Europe that it becomes a surprise to learn that their language was written in Cyrillic up until the nineteenth century and that Stephen the Great would have spoken Slavonic as well as Romanian.

*   *   *

For a few days I wandered between the churches, to Suceviţa, Moldo-viţa, Dragomirna, Arbore, Humor, Voroneţ. The rolling hills between them, the wide fields and the great deciduous forests, were still blowsy with summer.

I came to Suceviţa on a fine day when a few restless clouds cast quick shadows on the ground. The monastery church lay at the centre of a green quadrangle, enclosed behind fortified stone walls. Around it were meadows of long grass and clover. There I dozed through the middle of the day with the sun on my back, lulled by the bees and the crickets, listening to the clatter of geese and chickens in the nearby village, the bells of grazing livestock and the clop of horses on the road. Within the monastery, a nun beat out a prayer, circling the church and rhythmically striking a mallet against a wooden plank – bells were banned under Ottoman rule, since bells had traditionally summoned the population to battle, and for centuries the Tibetan sound of wooden hammering has been heard in their place. The beats came in double, triple time as they reverberated back from the walls of the great cloister.

Two nuns came out from a side entrance and turned towards the wooden houses of the village. They walked down through the tall grass starred with wildflowers, past a clump of white birches, seeming almost to float in their voluminous, slightly shiny, black habits.

Close before me was a little hollow where a spring bubbled into the monastic fishpond. The hay had already been scythed in the orchard on the other side. The cutters also lay on the grass eating lunch, talking and laughing in the shade of an apple tree. Two girls rose, two novices I supposed, in long black skirts with coloured kerchiefs tied over their hair. Languorous, hand in hand, they walked a short distance down the path made by two rows of heaped cut grass. Then dropped hands with a tinkle of laughter and wheeled away a filled barrow. They were gone. Light fell with too great clarity on the blue-green apple leaves, the silvery fronds of the young willow by the pond, the mirroring water.

Under the monastery walls the modern reality seemed near unbeliev-able.

At Dragomirna there were two foreign tourists besides myself. I walked by them as they sat in the courtyard with their backs against the sun-warmed wall of the church. They were in jeans, loose T-shirts and walking boots, yet were somehow classifiable as Eastern

Europeans. They greeted me in German and I sat down on the ground beside them.

Dragomirna too was fortified, behind high walls with square towers at the corners, and the monastery buildings were pitched against the walls on two sides. This church was of dressed stone, not painted on the outside, long and narrow as a keyhole, with an elaborately carved stone tower. The monastery was restored, clean, prosperous. In the courtyard the nuns had made a simple garden with clipped box bushes, roses and white tobacco plants; by the well, young birch trees gave a flutter of shade. An aged nun, head nodding, was carried out from the church by two of her young sisters with hands clasped to make a seat for her.

The Germans were students from East Berlin and had spent the whole summer holiday travelling in Romania, walking mostly, hitch-hiking when there was a car, sometimes taking trains. Rainer had a long apostle face, pony tail and transparent-rimmed spectacles; he talked earnestly in the ponderous phrases with which German tends to translate into English. Gerda was lighter and quicker. She had short blonde hair and wide green eyes, and sat with her broad face upturned to the sun.

'You know what is the best thing to be in this country?' she asked. 'A nun. As long as you sit here everything seems all right. Beautiful . . . But no, I could not be a nun. I could not forget the rest. Or be so friendly with Ceauşescu. In one monastery we went to we looked through a door into somebody's office and saw a big picture of Ceauşescu over the desk.

'Do people talk to you like they talk to us? In Transylvania we met many German people and every one had a story. They talk to us because we are German also but foreign. They tell us what they are too afraid to say to each other. How their families are divided, how they are not allowed to leave the country, how their children cannot speak German in school, what bad times their sons have in the army, how they cannot find work when they come out: even twenty packs of Kent cigarettes for the foreman will not help. They say they are hungry and they are afraid of the winter. We met a woman working in the mountains. She talked about the winter: what to do when it is below freezing, when there is nothing in the fields – let alone in the shops? When there is no work for the children to do?'

Gerda, herself coming from the East, was as shocked as I by what she saw in Romania. 'I come from DDR. I know that Socialism does not work, but it does not have to be like this!'

She talked of the disaster of Romanian agriculture, neglected while heavy industry had been developed, and how all the produce of the rich soil now went abroad to pay off industry's debts. As for the industry, there was a joke in Romanian: someone had told her that the word for 'state' was the same as the word for 'standing around'; thus a state factory was a place where people stood around all day. That was little different from East Germany: one man working for nine who stood idle, and for the one who did work the job was still a vacation; the real work began after he got home, on the black economy. But in Romania 'this normal Socialist phenomenon' had developed insane proportions. 'On a train we talked with a man who works in a big rubber factory, making tyres. Have you noticed that of the few cars on the roads, half of them are always mending punctures? And you know the big trucks that have two or three sets of paired wheels? We have seen some which have tyres only on alternate wheels.

'I tell you why. This man we met works on a production line. His machine makes some process which takes seven minutes. But the factory is making an economy on power: for every five minutes of electricity they have twenty minutes off. So he can never complete the process.'

An old nun with a parchment face and drooping brown eyes came up to us where we sat. She poured wine into a big glass for us to share, then came again with three pieces of cake – and the bottle, seeing how fast the wine went down. The cake was a honeyed mush of grains dotted with turquoise and pink sugar balls – called 'dead man's cake', I learnt later, traditionally shared out at the church or cemetery six months after a funeral. Rainer ate his in a second. 'I do not know why it is but that was the best thing I have eaten in weeks. Although perhaps I would not find it so delicious at home. It is hard to enjoy any food here. Hard enough only to find it.'

He asked if I had noticed the Sunday offerings that had been displayed in the church that morning. 'Did you see the bread? Beautiful fine white loaves, plaited, golden on top. I had never before seen such bread in Romania.'

'That is bread people make themselves,' Gerda said. 'You never see it in the shops. And the good white flour must come from the black market.'

*　　*　　*

We walked through the old orchard outside the monastery, across a field to a green lake. Behind us were the walls, pierced high up with a line of arrow slits.

Why had they come to Romania for the summer?

Rainer spoke. 'For us, this is the most interesting country we can visit, for the culture and for the land. Otherwise we have only Czechoslovakia, Hungary, Bulgaria. Even Poland is difficult for us to visit.'

'And Russia?'

'Russia is even more difficult. They have much bureaucracy and want everyone to go in a group. The Russians always go in groups.'

'Like the Japanese.'

'The Japanese go in groups also? That is interesting. But it may be the only characteristic that the Japanese and the Russians have in common.'

He had been to Romania a couple of times before, on walking holidays in the Făgăraş mountains. Each time he found less food, more poverty. The last year he had thought he would not come again, but Gerda had wanted to see and, then, it was perhaps good to know what was going on. There was little information on Romania in the East German newspapers; they heard more on West German radio, but not much. Even inside Romania, nothing was known for sure, but there were rumours. For example, they had heard that there was a meeting of dissidents a year before, in Piteşti or Ploieşti, one of the big industrial towns in the plain close to Bucharest. A group of writers and intellectuals met to discuss all the possibilities for change. None of them came home.

How many people?

'I don't know. Twenty, perhaps. I do not think they are the only ones. Many have curious accidents, fall under trains.'

'Why is it so important to you to know?'

He thought for a moment. 'Perhaps because it is a reflection. What might be.'

Beside the lake was the cemetery. The graves were drowning in long grass, meadow cranesbill, buttercups and wild celery.

'Come with us for a few days. It will not cost you much. We will camp, walk a little, take a train – and that costs no more than ten *lei* a ride. Only fools buy tickets here, the conductor is happy if you slip a ten *lei* note into his hand.'

But they were going towards Suceviţa, back the way I had come.

My visa did not give me time to dawdle more. There was, besides, the bicycle.

White geese roamed about the Moldavian villages, down the middle of the road in pompous processions of three or four, orange beaks in the air. The lush verges and wide village greens must have offered good pickings.

In the open fields between Dragomirna and the town of Rădăuţi, in the flatter land towards the Russian border, cabbages were being harvested. Outside each house and compound was a great wooden vat full of new cabbages put to pickle, the tops of the white globes not yet sunk beneath the weighted lids. Against half-filled vats the cabbages lay in piles, with a heap of the stripped green outer leaves beside them.

The houses had carved bargeboards and porches and sometimes elaborate glazed verandahs. Many were painted, their walls patterned with simple motifs like those of the peasant furniture, in sunny yellows and greens. One or two had pieces of mirror set into the walls to catch the light. Their yards were bright with flowers and often the wells had little roofs that were carved or latticed and painted.

Along the roads were large shelters, big enough to keep dry thirty people waiting for a bus or a gang of workers coming with their lunch from the fields. I did not know quite why they were put there but it seemed that every town and collective rivalled the next in their design. Local carpenters had been free to improvise wooden bandstands, kiosks and summer houses, wonderful structures fit for the grandest Victorian park.

Bandstands on country roads and village verges planted with flowers. Somewhere there must have been a propagandist dreaming of a sentimental peasant Communism. In a local museum I saw a poster from the early years after the war: a peasant couple stand at the base of a yellow-brick road looking towards the horizon where the sun is rising. Its yellow rays fan out behind misty factory towers. The colours are sugary pastels, baby blues and creamy yellows; the young peasants have huge limbs like the heroic figures on the early Soviet posters, yet their features are gentle and soft.

It was a stormy day when I began to climb again into the mountains and back into Transylvania. Some of the roads were so empty that I could go an hour without hearing a motor, yet at hairpin bends I found children holding out forest mushrooms to sell. They watched dully as I panted past. They must have walked miles from their villages and could hope to earn little in a day's foraging.

11

Sighişoara has the high, tight clustered roofs of an engraved Nuremberg or Augsburg. (You think of Dürer, only to learn that his father, a goldsmith, was born near Oradea, on the edge of Transylvania.) The citadel is on a hill, ringed by walls which climb steeply around it; at each crook and turn stands a narrow turret with triangular red roof. Within the outer walls rise the points of Gothic spires, the knotted tower of the main gate, and on the summit the brooding bulk of the Bergkirche.

It is a German town with the old German name of Schässburg, one of the original Siebenbürgen, the fortified towns established in Transylvania in the twelfth and thirteenth centuries by immigrants from Saxony. Like the Hungarians and Szeklers, the Saxons came at the invitation of the Hungarian kings, receiving freedoms and privileges in return for military service in the precarious and underpopulated eastern marches. Their independent burgher communities were swelled in the centuries that followed by later waves of German colonists, many brought under Habsburg rule to further strengthen the border against the Turks.

The old streets were bare and neglected, the cobbles glossy with rain. A few gipsies hung about, and the odd beggar, but not the medieval maimed – if such there ever were in Schässburg's prime. A crone in black kerchief sheltered in a doorway offering for sale a basketful of fresh mint in neatly tied bunches. Others like her had spread out cloth-wrapped bundles of wild mushrooms on the broad window sills of the post office, pale, saucer-like mushrooms and slim caps the colour of amber. At the bakery I queued for bread behind a man who was barely four foot tall, tiny but dignified in brown corduroy peaked cap, jeans and tweed jacket, with a dark cane in his hand: Rumpelstiltskin with a face like a dried apricot and sky-blue eyes.

It made sense that the Pied Piper was once credited with bringing the Saxons to Transylvania. You could picture the Piper jigging through the town gates. The story went that the children of Hamelin whom he lured into the mountainside were conjured a thousand miles to the east by some subterranean channel and released at last here in the Carpathian hills. One of the earliest sources of the legend, and the one which is supposed to have inspired Browning's poem, is a curious collection of Saxon myth and history published in the Lowlands early in the seventeenth century, by a recusant writer called Richard Verstegan. Verstegan reported that the surnames of the burghers of Hamelin reappeared frequently in the names of Transylvanian families. He repeated the explanation he had heard in Saxony, which concerned the Piper's necromancy, but went on to doubt its reliability on the grounds that there appeared to be no corroboration in Transylvania itself: he reasoned that people there must surely have kept a memory of so wondrous an event as the appearance of one hundred and thirty blond children out of the blue – 'if indeed any such thing had there happened.'

I climbed to the citadel, up a twisting road to the roofs and turrets that reared crookedly above. The clock tower at the gate had a gallery beneath the spire from which you could look out over still streets. In the room behind was the gigantic mechanism of the town clock, which brought out a figure at midnight to represent each day of the week. Only the wrong figure appeared to be out that day: it looked like Woden reviewing a decayed Schässburg on a drizzling Thursday. I checked, counting round from the sun-faced Sunday. A warlike Thor still waited in the wings.

A wooden tunnel covered the staircase to the Bergkirche, dry, dim, with grey light strained through oak slats. The church was fourteenth century, long-roofed, squat-towered. The tall windows were broken, covered with chicken wire and creepers. There was a cobweb across the curling handle of the door in the south porch, and the other doors were locked as well. Pale yellow leaves dropped from the linden trees around the church; I noticed how lindens turn quite suddenly, twig by twig going from green to pure yellow.

At a house close to the foot of the staircase a girl stood in the porch contemplating the rain. I stopped just to ask if it was possible to visit the church and stayed a long time talking. 'It is sad today, this town,' she said. 'You should be here another time.' There was a clump of yellow heleniums beside the porch, with petals turned back from drooping brown heads. 'Another time, the flowers there are like little suns. Come, I show you something.'

She led me across the yard hung with vines and purple grapes, up a rough path to a door in the battlements. She unlocked it and took me through a passage to a bastion garden. 'In summer I can sit here all day long.' The rain held back now. We leaned against the damp wall to look across the town. Reddening tendrils of Virginia creeper just reached the top of the wall; below the ground fell sharply, planted with fruit trees. From a lower bastion rose a top-heavy turret like a helmet askew on a twisted neck.

I asked if she had ever read Grimm.

'When I was a child I thought that tower down there was Rapunzel's tower. I did not know that you read the same in England.'

She told how the town was changing. Already the Germans were a small minority; there were many Hungarians in Sighişoara and now an increasing number of Romanians. Everyone she knew was leaving. Soon more of the native Germans would have gone to West Germany than would remain here, and then these old buildings would not matter any more. In May, emigrants from Sighişoara had held a reunion in a town near Stuttgart. Twelve hundred came. They had sent back a newsletter to Sighişoara.

Would she go too?

So far, her family had waited seventeen years for passports. They didn't know why it was taking so long. Perhaps it was because they had a close connection with the church. Others had waited twenty, twenty-two years. Most were luckier: all four of her mother's sisters had got to Germany after waits of between eight and fifteen years. She was in her early twenties; almost all her life she had been waiting. Now she was trying another way. Her fiancé had applied six years before but perhaps his family would have it easier. Then she could apply to leave to join him; where marriages were concerned two years was generally the maximum delay.

'When my parents first applied to leave, Romania was wonderful compared with now. Even ten years ago. More every year we dream of how it will be in Germany.'

'But isn't it hard for the old people to go? All their roots are here.'

'Oh no. That is nothing. Much better for them to go than to stand in queues on tired legs. Sometimes they must stand all day to buy food. And in winter, when the shortages are worst, they must go and stand out in the snow before it is light. Do you know about the winters here? Last year, the weather was not so bad, but two years, three years ago, it was a calamity. For days the temperature was minus thirty to thirty-five degrees.' She gave a momentary laugh, described how everyone in the house huddled around one wood-burning stove, told stories by candlelight. Heavy snowfalls had brought down power lines and caused long power cuts, night and day, and the gas pressure had sunk so low that they had no gas for cooking or heating water. 'But we got through. We live, you see!'

Before we parted I asked if there was nothing they could do to speed the papers along – a little money, a few dollars here or there. 'No, no. They would be afraid to take it. And we are not allowed to have foreign currency; perhaps they would tell. No. All we can do is wait.'

I went back to the church through the cemetery. The graves, set on terraces up the hillside, were beautifully tended, planted around with flowers. The stones were a record of the German community. The worn sandstone slabs of long-dead burghers lined the sides of the paths; they had been taken up from the graves and replaced by more recent stones dating from 1850 onwards. Marble and granite slabs, obelisks and urn-topped tombs all bore German names in Gothic script: Albert Ambrosius; Daniel Binder, *apotheke*; Julius Graef, *hotelier*; Maria Frank; Hans Schullerus; Julie Wagner. Soon these would be the only Germans left.

The girl had said that the church was normally closed. Some masonry had fallen from the roof and it had been declared unsafe for services, though nothing was being done about restoration. But it was possible to visit, and the woman who lived in the tower at the top kept the key. I found the crumbling turret with a washing line and a vegetable patch outside. I knocked and the door was answered by a dainty, fresh-faced old woman. '*Nein*,' she said instantly, she had no key, and moved to close the door. I persisted, but diffidently, reached for some money to offer for the church. '*Nein ist nein ist nein*,' she screeched, and slammed the door in my face.

On the other side of the town the streets dissolved into the beechwoods that spread over all the surrounding hills. I went for a walk in the dripping woods that afternoon, saddened by the town, and came back at sunset. Along the track went a man bent low beneath the rough bundle of branches on his back. In the distance rose the medieval walls. Gathering firewood: it was an autumn labour from a Book of Hours.

*   *   *

The villages in this district were like those of Hungary. The low houses had red roofs and walls washed in soft colours. Many had a Gothic church at the centre or on a hill above, a church fortified with high surrounding walls and look-outs as well as bell tower – for the independence of the early settlers was founded in the face of the Mongol and Turkish threats. The dusty streets were sleepy in the daytime, populated by the old and by foraging geese and turkeys. In the evening the sun put a glow on the houses: ochre, turquoise, blue. As I went east on the road leaving the village of Biertan the sun lit the scarlet tassels on horses' bridles and the faces of workers coming in from the fields.

The hills behind were cut with terraces but many of these were neglected, even abandoned. In the valley at Biertan old vines were swamped by twining weeds and golden rod. More than one Romanian had complained to me about the poor quality of the wine nowadays: once these districts had produced good Riesling but the German landowners had long since left, the vineyards were uncared for, and anything half-drinkable went for export.

It was in Biertan that I met Anna. She was one of a group of tall, pony-tailed girls coming out from the church. I stopped by them to ask if there was a camp site in the next town.

'Only a hotel,' she said in English. 'But you can come and stay with me.' Anna kissed her friends goodbye and we walked to her family's house on the edge of the village, she wheeling my bicycle, I carrying the prayerbook she had had in her hand. Anna was just out of school but poised as a madonna, with heavy, straight dark hair that fell forwards from its ribbon across her long face. She was going to start work soon in a factory in the town, though she didn't much want to. She said that when she got to Germany – for her family were all going to Germany – she would study some more. Or she would work in a kindergarten, 'like your Diana', and pronounced the name with a short 'i' and long 'ah'. Like who? 'Your princess.'

Herr Melzer, her father, was a carpenter, a long, quiet man who sat folded into a kitchen chair. Her mother sat at the table sorting plums into a huge tin bowl. When I arrived, she went to the mirror by the door, tidied her grey bun and tied a paisley-pattern scarf over it in deference to a visitor. She made me a cup of rosehip tea sweetened with honey, and gave me homemade bread with butter and deep red rosehip jam. Then, as her husband mused, she spread out on the tabletop another bagful of plums.

Plums soon heaped the bowl on the table. Anna picked out for me a handful of the finest, the colour of claret beneath a blue bloom. But these were only the leftovers from the day's bottling; on the step outside the door a row of filled jars stood cooling. Anna said the fruit had come from a neighbour's tree, swopped for grapes from the vine that overhung their yard.

All evening we sat in the whitewashed kitchen as Frau Melzer worked. When the plums were done she started a batch of bread. She had a rota with the neighbours by which each household baked on allotted days. I looked around the shelves. Almost nothing came from Romanian shops. Frau Melzer had herself gathered the rosehips for jam and tea: 'You must wait until they're very red, then dry them in the sun; and steep them overnight in water before boiling them up.' The honey came from a friend. Vegetables and fruit were grown in the garden or bartered in the village. The flour had been sent by a relative from Germany, as had sugar, coffee and other staples in the catering-size tins on the dresser. She said they managed well enough. The only problem was getting meat.

'Do you bake your bread in England? No? Then of course your mother does?' It was an old self-sufficient community she belonged to. She began to knead the dough, up to her pink elbows in flour. Her face was pale, plain, worn, but fine in Puritan terms: it looked honest and good.

She asked me about myself: about family and husband, whether I had children, about my religion, what I did with my days. I had to tell her that my father had died shortly before I set out on my journey, and was struck by her reaction. Anna was playing some music on a tape recorder – Cliff Richard, I think, in my honour – but her mother hushed her instantly and apologised: 'I am so sorry, if we had known we would of course have asked you first.'

'No,' I told her, 'the music's fine.' Yet envied suddenly the old solemn period of mourning instead of the hasty turning away into action and distraction now customary at home. In this world there was time for silence.

The Melzers did not talk politics. The first of the family had settled in Transylvania three hundred years earlier. 'It was a mistake' was all Herr Melzer said about it. 'Many Germans now think their ancestors made a mistake in coming.' Now, like everyone else, they were biding their time. It was Anna's brother who was most desperate to leave: he was currently doing national service and, as Anna said vaguely, if you're German and you've put your emigration papers in, you have a hard time in the Romanian army. Whenever he wrote he pestered them for news: had the first set of papers, which preceded the final set by a few months, come through yet?

I slept in the son's bed in the connecting room – the house was a long rectangle, and each white, low-ceilinged room ran through to the next. I went to sleep early, feeling drowsy and secure. Later I half-woke as someone tiptoed through, feigned sleep as Frau Melzer straightened the blanket and tucked me up.

12

I left in the morning with a kiss on each cheek and a call of God go with you! In my panniers, a fresh loaf, a bunch of sweet green grapes off the vine and a bag of dried rosehips for tea.

The road ran west to Sibiu along a broad valley. Though it had rained early in the morning, by ten the day was set fine and clear. But as I approached the town of Copşa Mică I found myself heading into a grey cloud. I had noticed it at first from a distance, a charcoaly smudge hanging between the hills. Gradually the cloud grew more distinct until it touched everything around; the leaves of the poplars along the road darkened and the creases in their bark became black with grime. I stopped to wipe a few specks of soot from my glasses and saw that my hands were becoming black as well.

It reminded me how Gerda, sitting in the monastery at Dragomirna, had talked about environmental problems in Romania, talked with a vehement Greenness that echoed the Germans of the West. She spoke of the dumping of toxic waste producing dioxins in the Danube delta, the subsequent isolation of the town of Sulina and the rumours of ecological disaster in the bird-rich delta land around it. Then she mentioned more general pollution. 'We saw a town that was all black, the houses and the people, with a black cloud above it. And once we came to a town that was white with white dust.' I had not thought then to ask the names of these biblical towns but they had come this way and I guessed now that the black one was Copşa Mică.

The prevailing west wind carried the pollution ten kilometres or more up the valley. Closer to the town the smudge was transformed into inky clouds; the crops in the fields were black, and black seedpods hung from grey-leaved acacias. The slogan at the town's edge was so dirty it was hard to read.

It was as Gerda had said. Everything was black, and the people on the streets had soot in the creases of their faces. They still grew maize

in the little fields between their black houses – what choice in Romania?
– but each leaf blade was black and curled at the edges. Through an
open gate I saw a flash of yellow. Someone had planted a flowerbed
with sunflowers, double sunflowers with thick-petalled globes. I looked
in, asked the woman on the porch if I could take a photograph: I was
so glad of the colour that I wanted to remember. She was flattered.
The sunflowers were very special, she told me, purely ornamental and
not used for seeds. And they had been sent to her all the way from
Germany.

'Everything else here is black!'

'I spray them with water or they would not be yellow for long.
Come and see. I have tomatoes, pimentos, cucumbers, all black. We
must wash these well before we eat them. See: if I rub the skin there
is the colour underneath.'

'Is it always like today? Look how black my hands are, and I've only
just arrived.'

She laughed. 'But you have smuts on your face as well!'

I tried to rub them off with a handkerchief but she only laughed the
more. I must have made it worse. 'How do you ever get clean?'

'We wash. All day we wash. Our bodies, our clothes, our food, the
flowers. Why, I do not know. Before we finish everything is dirty
again.' The absurdity of the conversation sent her into a mad peal of
laughter. 'And how do you think we dry the laundry? In the air, but
the air itself is black. All smuts!'

Copşa Mică's importance as an industrial town is founded on a source
of natural gas. Among other things, the gas is used to produce carbon
black, the black in dyes and printing ink and tyres. Romania is one of
the world's major suppliers of carbon black. I assume that this was the
job of the great black plant I saw with the belching smokestacks. But
can it have been efficient? How much of the product remained to be
bottled or packaged or whatever it is they do with carbon black? Surely
most of the stuff went on the wind?

In Sibiu I went straight to the Hotel Bulevard. I saw myself in the
mirror behind the reception desk: black as a chimney sweep despite an
attempt to wash off the worst at a village pump under the eyes of a
trio of giggling children. The Bulevard promised hot water. The foyer

had the trappings of an international hotel, down to a row of electric clocks announcing the time in Buenos Aires, Washington, Munich, Bucharest, Paris and Tokyo: except that all of them had stopped, victims of the austerity measures.

I asked at the desk if the room had a hot shower.

'Yes', the woman said, 'I think you might like one?'

I explained I had come through Copşa Mică.

'That was what I thought when you came in.'

'It's terrible. Completely black. Have you seen it?'

'Oh, it's been like that for years. The first time you go it's a surprise. For you or me, it would be a problem to live there, but the people in the town are used to it. They don't notice any more.'

The town square at Sibiu on a Sunday morning: religion and news-papers, like any warm square across continental Europe. Maybe it was just the September sun, but this was the first Romanian town I had come to that did not seem to be in a state of siege. A pattern of pedestrians flowed across the wide Piaţa Republicii, chased by their long shadows on the cobbles. Solitary men yawned and smoked and scanned the papers; others walked by wheeling bicycles. A flight of pigeons took off and scattered overhead.

The houses watched with half-closed eyes in their tall red roofs, the curved and elongated dormer windows of Germanic central Europe. Some looked older than their baroque fronts, irregular medieval build-ings shrugged into symmetrical façades. Through their massive wooden doors were vine-covered courtyards with flats that led haphazardly off stairs and galleries, and always a wrinkled grey head peering down to see who came below.

The bell tolled in the baroque tower of the Catholic church on the sunny western side of the square. Neat families and old women in buttoned cardigans converged towards it. A gate with another bulbous tower led to a smaller arcaded square, and beyond this rose the spire of the Lutheran church. While most of the later German settlers who came under the Habsburgs were Catholic, the descendants of the original families of Sibiu – or Hermannstadt, one of the oldest of the Siebenbürgen – are Lutheran. Their church is Gothic, worn and imperfect, expanded and transformed over five centuries. It gives an impression of mass, not light. Heavy grey stone piers line the nave, and high up between them, carved memorials weigh on the eye; they seem like encrustations on the side of an underwater wreck, heaped into scrolls, acanthus leaves, shields and skulls.

The Romanian Orthodox cathedral is upstart by contrast, not even a hundred years old. I found it later, a little way from the old town centre. The wide dome was filled with an oily light that came through yellow windows. A mass baptism was in progress, a dozen squalling babies simultaneously being blessed, stripped, bathed, named, anointed and photographed by hustling professionals. The ceremony looked improvised though it must have been ancient, switching between secular chaos and high ritual. Throughout it, relatives and onlookers milled sociably around. Many wore the stiff, surprised look of country people unused to city clothes. Unlike the bourgeois Germans, ordered in their oak pews, these families can have been in the town little more than a generation.

After church sedate groups went to the park where old men played chess and backgammon, or strolled on the old ramparts. ('Look at that!' a German frau hissed with appalled respectability, leaning on her husband's arm, and pointed at a peroxide blonde who lolled against a wall, showing almost the entire length of a black-lace leg through the slit in her satiny yellow skirt.) Most of Sibiu's youth seemed to be gathered outside the cinema: the Sunday matinée was *Simon Templar Intervines*, starring Roger Moore, followed by *Cat Ballou*, excitingly billed as an Oscar-winner of 1965.

The history museum had a display on local industry. Organised chronologically, the museum took the visitor from ancient Dacia (illustrated with quotations from Herodotus, Thucydides and Ceauşescu) to the present day via the usual peasant revolts and nationalist uprisings and the 'liberation struggle' in which the *Conducator* Ceauşescu figured as a blurred figure in the background of vastly blown-up newspaper photographs. The final room and the biggest was devoted to his 'heroic epoch'. In glass cases stood model trucks and bulldozers of a technological perfection never seen on the roads; on the walls were photographs of mammoth industrial plants, shipyards of shining steel and white-coated technicians in huge computer rooms. Graphs and diagrams gave a graphic picture of the country's progress: for example, the supply of electricity soaring up on a rocket-like trajectory from 1965 to 1987. And beside the door hung an ornate chandelier made in the local glassworks; there was an illuminated light bulb on every one of its half-dozen convoluted arms. It was the first fully stocked chandelier I had seen in the country.

In the little gallery where local artists sold their work, I met a woman who had been to Kensington.

'You come from London? What part of London?'

'Islington.'

'Is that near Kensington?'

'No, it's the other end of the city.'

'So have you not been to Barker's? I stayed with my friend in a square just behind Barker's. My friend is married to an Englishman.'

She was middle-aged, with too large earrings and too plucked eyebrows. I looked for the little dog that should have yapped at her heels, and decided she must have left it at home. Perhaps it was a cat.

'Do you paint?' I asked.

'A little. You know, for us artists this is a meeting place. I come here often. Though, of course, Sibiu was once a much more lively place than it is today.'

'Why is that? Is it because everyone's leaving?'

She might not have heard the question. 'But you must see our work. In particular, these paintings on glass are by a most talented girl, don't you think?' She dragged me enthusiastically across the room. 'Did you know that painting on glass is a folk tradition here? This artist takes her ideas from peasant motifs and creates something quite original with them, don't you think?'

I followed her round politely.

'But what brings you to Romania?'

'I'm cycling from Vienna to Istanbul.'

'Why?'

'It's something I've always wanted to do.'

'Ah. How strange. Now, have you always lived in . . . that part of London you mentioned?'

'I grew up in the country. Not so far from Oxford.'

'Oxford? I visited Oxford. You have a famous cathedral there.'

'Not at Oxford. It's really known for its university.'

'How stupid of me! Of course, I was thinking of Bath. It was many years ago that I went to England and the places get a little confused.'

*   *   *

I escaped after half an hour. As I unlocked the bike in the arcade outside, a man came out from the gallery and looked around vaguely. He was a wisp of a man, dry-looking and brittle, with a boyish face and white hair that curled over his collar.

'Excuse me. Is it correct that you are going to Istanbul on this bicycle? I am sorry, I could not help but hear you talk.'

Hermann Frank introduced himself. He said he hoped I could understand his English; he had taught himself from books. 'I am autodidact. I teach myself many things. And English is not so difficult for us here. I have read that the syntax of our Saxon German is close to that of English, for we also come from the west of Europe, from the lowlands.'

He said that he too was a painter. There was a museum in the town with a wonderful collection of Dutch painting. He loved the still lifes there. He painted still life himself though it was becoming hard nowadays to find fruit good enough to paint – whatever got to the shops in the town was misshapen, bruised and scabbed. But he stopped himself. 'I am sorry, I am wandering – that is what you say is it not? Have you seen our beautiful churches in Sibiu? Can I take you there? I also have a bicycle.'

We went first to the Lutheran church. It was closed but Hermann knocked on the presbytery door and persuaded a man to open both the church and the spire for us. We climbed up cobwebbed metal stairs to the belfry, over downy feathers and the stinking debris of bats and pigeons. Hermann said that the great bell was donated by Simon Brukenthal, an eighteenth-century governor of Transylvania, whose son had built the baroque palace in the square and begun the picture collection. The staircase had been made by his own grandfather, early this century, to replace the original wooden one. His grandfather had been an engineer.

'Are you an engineer too?'

'No. I am a gardener. That also goes in the family. The uncle of my mother was a head gardener to the Esterházys. He came from Bohemia.'

At the base of the spire were four turrets, tiny polygonal rooms with a narrow window on each face. Their floors were deep in feathers and a crowd of surprised flies flew out when we opened the windows. Each one gave a new view of the town, its baroque centre, the industrial suburbs and the beginnings of building work there, the hills beyond. Hermann identified all the churches: the Catholic church in the Piaţa Republicii, built by the Jesuits, the slim spire, patterned in polychrome

tiles, of the Hungarian Calvinist church, the broad dome of the Orthodox cathedral; further off, in the lower part of the town, were the pretty
yellow Maria Theresien Kirche, the former Ursuline convent, a second
and earlier Orthodox church, and a towerless green building on the
shadow of the hill. This last I guessed was Baptist.

'They are newcomers here,' Hermann said – though Baptist missions
had been established in Romania in the first half of the nineteenth
century. 'They sing many hymns but their churches are very plain.'

He himself belonged to the Lutheran church. Some of his ancestors
had memorial plaques in the annexe, and he pointed out in the precinct
below us, just beyond the roof of the chancel, his grandfather's house
and, a few shuttered windows away, that of his grandmother's family. The
Franks were part of the history of Sibiu. When I mentioned the apparent
German exodus he said it was sad to see the others leave. The town would
die. For himself, he could not imagine living anywhere else.

On our bicycles we made a tour of the other churches – the few that
were open – save for the Baptists'. Hermann cycled slowly, bow-legged
and precarious.

We went to Sibiu's old almshouses, on the side of the steep hill that
dropped directly beneath the Lutheran church. They had been founded
by the church not long after the Germans had first settled the town
and had been in almost continuous use since though they were now
run by the state. Hermann announced to the toothless old men on the
bench by the gate that I was an *Englander* cycling to Istanbul. The
news spread through the medieval labyrinth of crooked passages and
galleried courtyards and brought out faces to greet me. Eighty people
lived there, the men on the outer courtyard, the women on an inner
one that was shaded by a lime tree and calm with an atmosphere of
purdah. Each individual had a dim cell with a metal bed and little other
furniture. Conditions did not seem to have changed much since the
place was built, except that the chapel was derelict, piled against its
wall a heap of rubbish that included the skeleton of a pony trap.
Hermann showed me the old greenhouses in the abandoned garden;
not a pane of glass was still in place. He said that fifty years before,
the old people had been able to grow things for themselves: how good
it must have been for them to occupy their time so.

We parted in the modern square by the Hotel Bulevard. I invited
him to eat with me. No, he said, every evening he went to his friend's
house where he had a room to paint in. I asked why he did not work
at home.

'My wife is there. It is not possible.' He shrank a little as he spoke. He added that she was his second wife. His first wife had thought only of children.

'Didn't you want children?'

'There is no reason to have children.'

'Does your second wife think that too?'

'No, we have a son, eighteen months old.'

'Do you spend time with him?'

'Not much. After work, I study, I paint. For that I must make time. I am, as I have said, autodidact.'

I wondered if Hermann had wanted to be the last of the Franks.

'Do you think the Germans would leave if things were different? No. They just look for the easy life. Romania's problems are theirs as much as ours.'

At the camp site, where I had moved after a single clean but expensive night at the hotel, I had breakfast with my Romanian neighbours. Radu was one of the Bucharest middle class, a construction engineer. His family came from Moldavia. They had been rich once, he said. Why, his grandfather had sold a million eggs and bought a Rolls Royce: think how much land he must have owned to have chickens enough to produce a million eggs. (All at once, in a month or a year? I should have asked.) Were they boyars? No, he laughed, did boyars keep chickens? But he had a look of the boyars in sixteenth-century portraits, dark-cloaked figures full-length in glistening oils. He had broad, hard-cut cheekbones; his hair receded on his flat skull and his beard was trimmed into a fine outline along the jaw, around the wide lips and up the centre of the chin.

He lounged in a folding chair while his girlfriend, Doina, brought out tin after tin of imported food from the boot of the car: Chinese Seagull-brand cocoa and Nescafé, Chinese milk powder, Russian luncheon meat, Russian liver pâté. The plum jam she had made herself; it was not very good. She was pert and urban, would have been more at home in the West with a microwave. She complained how much work had gone into stocking up for the holiday, a year of haunting the shops at dawn and asking for things that were never seen on the shelves in the hope that they might appear from beneath the counter.

Around us, most of the other campers had left early. Eastern European camp sites sometimes seemed more like transit camps.

Tourists would come like refugees in the middle of the night, on foot, carrying small suitcases and plastic bags, and go off to sleep in numbered huts. In the morning they would leave as mysteriously. Others, like the Poles encamped on the far side of my tent, set up both home and shop in their caravans, cooked enormous meals and drank and sang half the night. Now these too were moving on. Gone was the little queue that had formed outside their caravans each morning – camp-site cleaners and local women come to buy their black-market goods that ranged from coffee to deodorants, lace stockings and children's toys. Two battered old Mercedes had to be coaxed into action, the first one left to tick over while its driver tinkered beneath the bonnet of the second. At last both panted off with a puff of foul exhaust.

Radu watched scornfully. 'In the summer the Poles are like gipsies. You find them everywhere. They show off in their Mercedes-Benz but Poland's no richer than we are. They are allowed to travel, that's all, so they deal their way around, down to the beaches on the Black Sea. Buy something in one country, sell it in the next. Petrol coupons, anything. They're so greedy for a profit they'll even siphon the petrol out of their tanks, then wait for a tow from the next Pole along the road.'

He lit a West German cigarette and went on with a wild chauvinism. He said how the Romanians deserved sympathy from the West far more than the Poles or Hungarians. They were the most persecuted of the peoples of Eastern Europe. But he was talking not so much of the present day as of the country's entire history.

'The Romans called our country Dacia Felix. That was one of the only times it was happy.' He lectured me on Transylvania, reversing all I had heard in Hungary. The truth was that the Hungarians had been there not a thousand years – a snap of the fingers; and all that time it was the Romanians who were the majority, though they had had no vote until the 1860s and though they had been forced to learn Hungarian. 'Do not believe what the Hungarians told you.'

I thought of the didactic display in the town museum: there had been blown-up photographs of the Dacian prisoners depicted on Trajan's Column and alongside, photographs of Romanian peasants in traditional dress, with large and educative arrows pointing out similarities in their thigh-length tunics, tight trousers and thonged leggings. There had been no need to read the captions to follow their drift: the direct descent of Romanian peasants from the Romano-Dacians, and thus their prior claim to the Carpathian uplands disputed by the Hungarians. In a popular burst of nationalism not long after he came to power Ceauşescu had had a life-size plaster copy of Trajan's Column made and shipped from Rome.

'The Hungarians are cold. They do not have heart like the Romanians. We are a gentle, Latin people. Our natural friends are in Western Europe, in France and Britain. The Romanians are cultured: look how easily they learn languages.' Radu explained my failure to find an English dictionary anywhere in the country as the result not of a paper shortage but of national linguistic achievement: the dictionaries were bought up as soon as they came off the press.

Breakfast went on a long time. Doina watched dully, stirring up a third cup of milk powder and Nescafé, while he marked a map of Romania on the ground and with sweeps of his broad hands indicated the historic encroachments of greedy empires: Mongol, Hungarian, Turk, Habsburg; and Russia ever waiting to pounce. But for all the truth in what he said I could not help picturing amidst the picnic mugs on the grass more blown-up photographs and schoolmasterly arrows. I was sceptical. I could not forget the fantasy with which the museum display had ended, with the glorified history of the great leader and his industrial wonderland. All Romanian history now seemed propaganda.

13

South of Sibiu lay the last stretch of the Transylvanian plateau, tinged with the colour of rust and buffeted by wind. Dark clouds were dashed across the sun; from them fell a few fat drops of rain that were instantly swept away. The haymaking was urgent now. I stopped to rest on a mown strip of grass beside a sea of maize; beyond the dry tossing stalks rose the Făgăraş mountains, sudden and blue as massed atolls. On the grass three women worked with rakes, their black skirts and scarves billowing, while three men loaded the cut hay on to carts. One of them shouted a greeting that reached me thin as an echo. The wind tore at the hay on the pitchforks and sent the loose piles on the carts streaming like blown hair.

The road entered the great gorge where the river Olt cuts through to the base of the Carpathians. The Olt flows fast through the mountains, due south, for almost a hundred kilometres and the road runs alongside, infinitesimally dropping as the Carpathians themselves dwindle towards the Danubian plain. That day, the gorge was a calm channel in the shelter of the flanking mountains. The wind no longer blustered, only weighed against me with a constant pressure that offset the gentle gravity of the slope. I pedalled slowly. The grey walls of rock above had a prison monotony, momentarily broken when a rift opened to the east and snowy peaks showed through it. There was no side road to take me to the mountains; no passage but the gorge slowly falling towards Bucharest.

The walls began to open out and I came to the Byzantine monastery of Cozia. It struck me as dark and small after Transylvania. No more Gothic height: this was Wallachia. Behind the low buildings, where the monks once meditated before a wild view, the river was crippled by a dam.

Călimăneşti was a famous nineteenth-century spa – famous at least in Romania, for there was never quite a Marienbad or a Baden-Baden here. Today the approach is cluttered with high-rise hotels where workers take packaged-holiday cures. The mineral springs are said to be effective for various cardiovascular, gynaecological and digestive ailments, for asthma, chronic bronchitis and arteriosclerosis, and also for 'industrial diseases'. Perhaps it was this last category which drew to the place so many limp track-suited bodies. They strolled along the yellowing avenues before the Hotel Central, sipping the smelly waters from little glass flasks, and wore on their faces the correct look of ennui, gazing blandly at the cinema programme pasted to the window of a pavilion. The Central was original, a grand nineteenth-century hotel studded with elaborate wooden balconies and bogus Transylvanian turrets. Inside, past a hall lit by an ostentatious modern chandelier (one bulb in twelve), were long panelled corridors where women in white coats brushed through creaking swing doors.

I went out again, sat on a leaf-strewn bench, read and reread the map. I saw then that I had slipped out of Transylvania by a back door. More than one Romanian had recommended the route: 'Take the Olt valley; it'll be a good ride.' But why? Just because it was flat? The day's ride had cheated me of the mountain tops, bringing me only that much closer to the urban and collectivised Romania of the plain.

At the base of the gorge was Rîmnicu Vîlcea. The old town had lost itself in the developments of the last two decades. Pedestrian figures swarmed on its broad institutional streets, so many people housed like termites in anonymous blocks where a family was represented by a line of washing on a concrete balcony. (Ceauşescu is said to dream of the day when every Romanian home has not only a washing machine but a tumble drier as well: how systematic his new towns will look then.)

In Rîmnicu Vîlcea I had difficulty buying bread. Not that there was lack of it – unlike some days in some towns when the bakeries had only wafers to sell to those who queued for their ration. Here for the first time the assistant refused to sell me anything since as a foreigner I had no ration slip at all. Only persistence won in the end, as I feigned total incomprehension and repeated my request ten times in English until those at the head of the fifty-strong queue lost patience and added their pressure to mine. 'Just this time,' the woman said starchily, reaching beneath the counter, not to the freshly stocked shelves behind her, and thrusting at me a day-old loaf.

But that grey bread lay heavy on the stomach. By now I was permanently hungry. I had finished the Debrecen salami weeks before and had been living on bread, tomatoes, peppers and onions like a good peasant, with the occasional tin of oily Yugoslav sardines for protein. Once I had found a shop selling Romanian salami and bought some with a sense of triumph, but it was soft and pale pink, gritty with crushed bone, and I could not eat it. Some marinated fish which I bought half-defrosted in a bare-shelved 'delicatessen' in Sibiu was fractionally more palatable though its flesh was the colour of lead. At least my dollar-based wealth could acquire for me a piece of fried meat and a handful of rice and chips in hotel restaurants – only in the biggest towns was more than one dish available – but the portions were small, measured out in grams, and to feel full at the end of the meal it was necessary to pack in a tasteless chunk of bread between each mouthful of meat.

Beyond the town was an eerie haze that seemed composed part of autumn and part of pollution. To the right the land rose under vineyards and orchards, grey earth planted in grey rows; on the flat ground to the left stood tall industrial chimneys and the hulks of factories. I followed a sign to the mountainside spa of Băile Govora, wondering whether I might not find something different for lunch.

Govora was a pretty provincial spa with buildings in Transylvanian art nouveau and terraced gardens of pollarded chestnuts and beds of marigolds. The strains of 'The Blue Danube' drifted down the avenues. A stiff military band played in the hexagonal bandstand, conducted by a squat and jolly officer. His audience was a score of small children in woolly hats – since the first of September every Romanian child seemed to have acquired a woolly hat. I found a refreshment house at the end of the walk, queued half an hour for some gristly kebabs and another half hour for two thick pancakes sprinkled with icing sugar. The entire population of the spa, grave peasant men and women with consumptive-looking children, appeared to be eating at the same two stalls.

It took a mere ten-minute wait to buy a coffee; the drink was ersatz but I no longer expected anything else. A television fixed high on the wall relayed the day's presidential speeches. The short grey figures of Ceauşescu and Elena flickered on a high dais above a staid multitude of delegates; Ceauşescu delivered a dreary litany of Latinate phrases among which I could recognise talk of modernisation and education, of the achievements of the *Epoca Luminoasă* or Era of Light. Then a blizzard hit the screen with a rude buzz and the picture was lost. The men at the table beneath the television came to life. Among them the military bandleader caught my eye.

'*Bună ziua*. Did you enjoy our music?'

'Very much.'

'And did you take a photograph?'

I explained that though I had taken my camera out it had been too dark under the trees for a picture – and remembered as I spoke the tourist information that expressly forbade photographs of the military.

His face fell beneath the gold-braided cap. 'The sun may come out this afternoon. Will you come back then and take one?'

Outside the grey clouds hung in unbroken banks. I had little hope for the washing strung on lines among the television aerials on the balconies of the old hotel. Two stout women in pink dressing gowns leant across the ornate metal railings on the fourth floor deep in conversation; it looked the sort of talk that flowed all day from bath to treatment room to balcony and back.

I had turned west a little way off the Bucharest road to see something of Oltenia, to visit the famous monastery at Horezu, said to be the masterpiece of Wallachian Brîncoveanu architecture, and also because I had an invitation from two local schoolteachers. I had met them in the market at Sibiu. The term had yet to start and the teachers had driven up with plums from the village to make a little money before-hand. Prices were fixed for each town and they reckoned to do better in Sibiu than in their own district or in Rîmnicu. Aurel told me he taught maths, a lanky young man who looked more a student than a teacher, with transparent-rimmed spectacles bandaged in tape. Stefan, neat, small and dark, taught French. They were unhesitatingly friendly in the market, and when I mentioned that I might be passing their village Aurel drew a map and told me how to find them.

Yet when I arrived I found that the roads did not conform to the map. Where Aurel had shown a left turn, I could see only a right. I circled and back-tracked and eventually took the road to the right; if the map was reversed it just about made sense. The first houses of the village appeared and then a school on the right like a mirror-image of the one the map indicated on the left. But no-one here knew of Aurel or Stefan, not the old woman who was passing by, not the children playing by the closed school gates nor the headmaster whom they called from his house. No, there was no Aurel Stoica or Stefan Costea at the school; never had been so far as he knew. There was an Aurel and he taught maths, a middle-aged man, a little plump, but his surname wasn't Stoica. Yes, this was Costeşti and there was no other village I would be likely to confuse it with.

I wasted an hour looking for them and gave up. Had I caught them off guard in Sibiu when I said I was going their way? The foreigner you chat with in a market a hundred and sixty kilometres away may not be the person you want to appear on the doorstep in the village where you live.

I tried to give point to the diversion by going on from Costeşti to a monastery up a rough road at the end of that valley. But the remote mountainside was raw with quarrying and a workers' barracks overshadowed the church; the trees around were dusty with blown gypsum from a cement works: it wasn't worth the journey. Up a parallel valley a short distance further on the great monastery of Horezu at least was unscathed, raising its high stone walls amid orchards and pasture where huge oxen grazed. I sat in the church, willing away the aimlessness that had come over me. Two nuns chanted an evening service, standing at lecterns either side of the nave. Their faces were shadowy in the candlelight that brought out only the gold haloes of the icons.

When they left the church I asked if it was possible to stay there the night. But that, it seemed, was a question for the Mother Superior. I waited a long time in the courtyard and at last she appeared. Like a headmistress with rich parents, she escorted to the gate a trio of dark-suited visitors. After a lengthy ritual of smiles and thanks they rolled off in a chauffeur-driven black Dacia. The pale nun then registered my presence and greeted me in elegant French. I remembered my ten years at convent school and spoke apologetically: I had missed the time; I was a woman alone; it was getting dark; could I pitch a tent in their orchard?

Her regret was perhaps a little excessive. 'How unfortunate that you are travelling so late. Of course, we would be so happy to help you but it is sadly quite impossible.' Her long fingers clasped piously; her eyes fixed on mine. 'I must tell you that there are wolves in these mountains. You would be much safer in a hotel. You will find one just a few kilometres further on.'

There was a peace here that I would not find at the hotel. A girl sat in a doorway peeling apples in perfect spirals.

'Surely the wolves do not come down so low at this time of year? I have camped many times before and most Romanians do the same . . .'

Her face was gradually hardening. 'You should take my advice. In England you are not accustomed to such dangers. And there are the bears. Really, the hotel will be far more suitable.'

'But bears are very shy creatures and there are many people in the monastery and the village to scare them away.' What next, I wondered, tigers?

I had driven her too far. The hands broke apart and came together with a smart clap. 'I am sorry, it is out of the question. I cannot permit you to stay here. It is the law. All Western tourists must stay in hotels; no camping of any kind is permitted.'

In the twilight I wheeled the bike a mile or so up the rutted and sandy track that cut across to the small town of Horezu and its unattractive hotel. A little further on I reached an isolated camp site whose token fence had long since begun to collapse. The sole visible inhabitant was a dog that stole by my tent in the middle of the night and snatched away an empty sardine tin and the other debris of my supper.

I covered the fifty kilometres back to Rîmnicu Vîlcea, where the main road went south to Bucharest. A single night on the way would leave me a week before my visa expired; time to see as much of the city as I wanted. Rîmnicu was still shrouded in mist. For breakfast – or lunch – I stopped at a stall on the street and had a couple of stale rolls filled with brown jam and a green ice-cream.

The two days since leaving Transylvania had been grey, lonely, interminable. I looked at the map yet again. I noticed a new road: a winding yellow road that climbed north-east from Rîmnicu in the direction of Braşov, crossing the grain of the sub-Carpathians, leap-frogging from valley to valley over ten rivers that poured south from the Făgăraş watershed. A couple of days' ride would reach Braşov, German Kronstadt; then I could leave Transylvania a second time by the high pass at Predeal. I could still be in Bucharest just within the time on my visa, and even if I got no extension it was only a three-hour ride from there to the Danube and the border. The yellow road was compelling. The way south was all too predictable.

The sun came out as I left the valley above the dammed Olt. From the top of the first long climb I found myself in a rich September light that set a fire on the beeches and the blond pasture, and on the stubble that supplanted the pasture as the land dropped again. On the next hilltop I stopped to pick blackberries from the high thickets that clustered along the roadside. There I met a band of picture-book gipsies. They had stopped to rest their horses after the climb while the drivers fixed old tyres to drag behind the waggons; a man's weight on these gave braking on the steeper sections of the descent. The gipsies were friendly and tried to talk but I could understand little of what they said. Except that they, if no-one else, seemed to show enthusiasm for my journey. '*Bravo!*' A handsome woman in gloriously bright skirts swung me round and clapped me on the back. She made me feel ludicrously happy, lucky and free.

I raced down, the wind roaring in my ears. I overtook the only motor I had seen in an hour, a juddering van that crawled fearfully round the bends.

When we were children we lived in a village at the foot of a hill. The other side, beyond the pub, the road dropped steep to a reservoir and rose again instantly towards the next village. We would shoot down it on our bikes, pedalling furiously for as long as we could, then lie still, flat against the handlebars, and see how far the impetus would carry us up the second hill. My brother usually won the challenge and once, as I wobbled to a halt, he glided right up to the top.

At dusk I came to a densely populated valley that offered little concealment for camping. I stayed instead in a village house. On the road I had stopped by two women who were dragging home a heavy trolley loaded with wood, humping it awkwardly over the ruts and stones. Each had pressed me to stay with her but it was the older one who had spoken first. Her name was Leica and she had a long stern face that curled like a wizened leaf when she smiled. She lived in a square newish house close to the river and the strip of poplars that ran along the edge of the village. It was not her own but belonged to a colonel stationed elsewhere; she looked after it and his family sometimes came for weekends. A military uniform and cap hung from a hook on the kitchen door. She put bread and tomatoes before me and watched me eat, asking questions. Where is your husband? Your children? Where are you going? Why do you go there? Why do you go alone? In the living room was a big wooden bed she made up for me to sleep in. From a chest she brought out a pink nylon nightdress that I hoped did not belong to the colonel's wife. A black-and-white regimental portrait hung on the wall, and a wedding photograph, twenty years old judging by the bride's bouffant hair. The only decorations besides these were embroidered swags of cloth hung above the doors and windows and over the mirror.

The dog at the gate barked and rattled its chain. Her friend, Vera, had brought her husband to visit. She had changed from her working clothes into a straight-cut woollen skirt and cardigan buttoned to the neck. Vasili, the husband, was buttoned up too and wore a beret jammed flat on his head. He greeted me with a glint of steely teeth and produced a couple of eggs from his pocket as a gift.

The three of them sat in a row at the table, stiff as puppets, as I tried, in my limited Romanian, to entertain them. Eventually I had the idea of bringing out my map to show them my route. Vasili, as the male taking the lead, put a hand to it and pushed it back and forth across the table with an air of understanding but I realised suddenly that a map was as meaningful to them as wallpaper. None had travelled further than the fifty kilometres to the town of Cîmpulung.

Every now and then one or another gave a great yawn, like a stubborn child who stays up too late. It was I in the end who had to make the move, point out what time it was. And they probably rose at dawn. Vasili took my address and wrote theirs down for me, laboriously drawing the loops and curls of each letter as he had been taught them as if every flourish were equally crucial to the meaning.

Leica cooked the eggs for my breakfast in the morning and I met Vera as I was leaving the village. She took down a basket from her head, placed it carefully on the ground and planted a resounding kiss on each cheek. In the early sunshine the road was lively with people fetching water from the wells, walking out to the fields or to the orchards on the hillsides to pick the apples and plums. Where a walnut tree stood on the verge they shook the branches and gathered the fallen green nuts. A couple of ridges further on, past alpine meadows smudged purple with clover, the land hardened into mining country. The two wide valleys before Cîmpulung were spanned by a giant pulley system transporting rusty buckets of coal that creaked mechanically overhead as I wound along the road beneath. Trucks rumbled by laden high and loosely with coal and leaving in their wake a litter of rocks and black dust.

After Cîmpulung the road turned more directly north through jagged limestone hills and ravines. Crags stood out among forests pricked with the needle outlines of pines, or reared up Chinese and shadowy in the half-distance. Clouds closed in the sky so that only for brief moments were the peaks to the west and east revealed, streaked with rivulets of snow.

The Guivala Pass started steeply from the ravine of the Dîmbovița at Rucăr and rose to more than twelve hundred metres. As I climbed I heard a sporadic rumble of army firing in the mountains. Its source was hard to pinpoint as I wove back and forth along the hairpin bends. There was almost no traffic and the throb of the guns was met only by the sound of my own breathing. Then, close to the top, I saw a group of soldiers lazing at the edge of a sparse wood of pine trees. A military truck came up behind and the soldiers brought out jerry cans to be filled with water. I greeted them and presented my own water flask, and the driver waited to fill it up again as I drank a first long draught. I told him the water was cold and beautiful, *foarte frumoasă*. 'Of course. It is mountain water.' The soldier had startlingly blue eyes.

I swooped down past the army camp and the firing range, past signs forbidding photography, past trees, then pasture and farms and mountain villages, to arrive bone-cold from the wind at Bran, where a castle guarded the narrow passage to Transylvania.

14

There was another foreign guest in the B-category hotel at Bran, also English, also a cyclist and from Islington, too. He had left Cîmpulung at midday and must have been just ahead of me all afternoon.

He had arrived in the country only forty-eight hours earlier, whirled at midnight by airport taxi into a blacked-out Bucharest, and had spent the two days on the road to Transylvania. He was here for a fortnight's holiday; the previous year he had gone to Tuscany and now he looked for something different. The newspaper stories about the destruction of the villages, which had put off many of those tourists who still remembered Romania, had only strengthened his determination to come: one might as well see what might so soon disappear.

He was beginning to wonder if the country wasn't a little mad. Coming from Cîmpulung he had had a strange encounter on the road. There was a buffalo cart he had passed, whose driver had yelled out a greeting or something; a little later it caught up with him as he stopped to smoke a cigarette. The driver handed the reins to the young boy seated beside him and got down to talk. The man was clearly drunk and it was only after much impassioned gesticulation that Peter realised what was the object of his interest: a Peugeot cycling shirt, body-hugging, shimmering sapphire and silver, with Peugeot written down the arms and across the chest. The man had fallen in love with it. He emptied his pockets of so many hundred-*lei* notes that Peter guessed he had just come from market, and seeing no sale, in desperation finally stuffed the great wad under his belt and offered to throw in his two fine buffalo: a bargain if ever there was one. But Peter was well-bred and fair-minded, a barrister at Lincoln's Inn. He looked at the boy watching wide-eyed on the cart and felt bound to refuse; he was travelling light, he needed his shirt, but more than that, it seemed that the boy's patrimony was at stake. At last the man drove off, sad and muttering. 'But for a moment I was tempted,' Peter said. 'Imagine driving down Upper Street in a buffalo cart!'

In the morning we looked at Bran Castle, which loomed grey and Scottish out of a mist. It was Peter who reminded me of its supposed connection with Dracula. I had almost forgotten Dracula, so irrelevant was his figure in the real Transylvania, no more than an Englishman's fantasy. An unfinished copy of Bram Stoker's book lay crushed beneath the tent in my bicycle pannier.

In name if in little else, Dracula was inspired by a fifteenth-century lord of Wallachia who is known in Romanian history as Vlad Tepeş, or Vlad the Impaler, though he also inherited from his father the name of Vlad Dracul, the Devil. Historical accounts portray Vlad as a man who had even the Ottoman sultan in awe of his diabolical cruelty. Impalements were apparently his answer to all the major problems of rule. He effectively silenced internal opposition, for a time at least, by inviting most of his boyars to dinner and having the guests skewered before him as he feasted at the high table. With the Turks he was marginally less successful. The sultan gathered together an invading army following Vlad's rash decision to impale an entire Turkish delegation in 1461, even though diplomatic protocol was said to have been observed in so far as the pasha who led the party was given the distinction of a stake higher than those of his subordinates. Closer to home, to combat what he perceived as economic exploitation by Saxon merchants, Vlad had some burghers impaled on a hill in Braşov – four hundred or thirty thousand of them, depending on which chronicle you read, some impaled belly-first and some the other way up, with the stakes neatly arranged in geometrical configurations. As for welfare, he is said to have declared that he would have no more poverty or disease in Wallachia and accordingly invited to a banquet all the beggars, gipsies and cripples in the land; when all had eaten well he had them burnt alive.

One wonders whether the simplicity of Vlad's solutions might not appeal to the current Romanian régime. It is interesting to observe that Vlad has recently been given a heroic status in Romanian national history. In truth, even reading from the most impartial accounts, he appears to have been a somewhat equivocal figure, sadistic puppet prince of a tiny buffer state between the Ottoman Empire and Hungary, in and out of power and changing sides as political expediency or his natural perversity dictated, who was finally and appropriately killed with the connivance of one of his own boyars during a campaign against the Turks. Yet the official myth now defines the accusations of cruelty as German and Hungarian slanders and sets Vlad up instead as a Crusader, a Robin Hood who gave to the peasants what he took from the boyars and the Saxons, and as an early Romanian nationalist. His strong links with Transylvania as well as with Wallachia – he was born in Sighişoara – his oppression of the Saxons and of the nobility and his brief assertion of strong centralised authority, to say nothing of his rough justice, must offer attractive historical precedents today. (A comparison can be made with the Soviet rehabilitation of Ivan the Terrible which took place in the mid-years of Stalin's rule.)

Coinciding with Vlad's ascendance has been a corresponding diminution in the prominence of Count Dracula in Romanian publications. Until the late 1970s Dracula was energetically promoted by the tourism agencies as a welcome source of hard currency. Since then, however, this tourist attraction has been played down. Presumably it is no longer considered amusing to treat a patriotic hero so, however many dollars he may bring in. Could it also be possible that the message 'Dracula lives' which has appeared on demonstrators' banners at protests outside Romanian missions abroad, and most notably during the Ceauşescus' 1978 visit to New York, has become a source of embarrassment to the Romanian leader?

Cloud hung low over Braşov, seeping down the sides of the mountains that enclosed the town. Rain veiled the long Austro-Hungarian streets, dulled even the paintpot colours of the main square. This had recently been renewed, repainted and repaved with civic thoroughness, laid out with sculptures and fountains, a couple of the medieval houses entirely reconstructed and converted into restaurants and cafés with smoked-glass windows. These would have looked quite cosmopolitan but for the drab queues that spread from their doors: a wet half hour was an obligatory preliminary to tea and a plate of sandwiches on cocktail sticks or of synthetic profiteroles. Braşov was once the home of a famous patisserie, someone had told me, which sold the finest cakes in all Romania, but suddenly one morning it vanished; rumour said that it did good business now in Tel Aviv.

I wondered if the renewal of the square had any connection with the riots that had occurred in Braşov almost a year before, if it represented an attempt to appease the populace with at least an appearance of cosmopolitan prosperity. The riots of November 1987 had been the most violent demonstration against the Ceauşescu régime in a decade. They had given rise to a flurry of dramatic stories in the Western press: five thousand, ten thousand, more than twenty thousand workers had marched into the town centre and ransacked the Communist Party headquarters, throwing desks and typewriters from the windows, burning Romanian flags and pictures of Ceauşescu, chanting 'We want bread' and 'Down with the dictator'. A couple of reports suggested that their anger was inflamed further by the discovery of stores of food in the building, even round cheeses and oranges – shocking luxuries that winter when meat and cheese were unavailable in the town and when even milk powder could be got for children only on doctor's prescription. It was said that at least one policeman was killed.

Yet almost as quickly as it had come, the story faded; a week later *The Times* reported that a Western diplomat visiting Braşov – for of course no journalists had been allowed there – could not confirm any damage to public buildings. It seemed an anticlimax.

At the time it had appeared that the riots could be the beginning of a wider revolt. Silviu Brucan, a former editor of the Party paper *Scînteia* and former ambassador to Washington, now forced into opposition, described the riots as a 'watershed'. (He found himself under house arrest from the beginning of December.) The dissident writer Liviu Cangeopol, in an interview with the Paris daily *Libération*, said that the event marked a point where Romanians recognised that they could be terrorised no further; on the walls of the city hall the protesters had scrawled 'We do not fear death.'

Little news came in the months that followed to clarify what had actually happened. It was known that the demonstration was led by workers from the huge, prestigious and unprofitable Red Flag tractor factory. The general resentment at austerity measures and food shortages, at new winter restrictions on domestic gas and electricity supplies, and at compulsory Sunday working, had boiled over there when twenty per cent pay cuts were announced. It was also clear that, whatever actual damage the riots had caused, they had swiftly been put down by the militia and a large number of people had been arrested on the spot.

The authorities, however shocked they might have been at what had occurred, seem to have been most efficient in their reaction. In public they applied a soft touch. Food supplies were rushed into the city and the workers were told that their demands would be granted. Local officials were publicly criticised and factory managers fired. An amnesty the following January enabled the release of many of those arrested in November, both at Brașov and in subsequent demonstrations elsewhere. But an uncertain number of others were not released. With the other hand, the authorities quietly began to retract what they had appeared to give. Red Flag workers found pay cuts reimposed. Hundreds of them were relocated, dismissed or disciplined. In March a lone report appeared in England that a woman who had been arrested at the demonstration and subsequently released had been found beaten to death in a park.

On the road somewhere on the way to Sighișoara, two men in a car had stopped to talk to me. Both worked as technicians in factories in Brașov, though they doubled as ski instructors in the winter months and thus spoke some English. They had passed me a few minutes before and guessed that I was a Westerner. What, they asked straightaway, did I think of Romania?

It was difficult to know what to say to such strangers, though these two seemed straight enough. Both were about my age, I guessed, in their thirties, the driver dark and pleasant-looking, the other slightly scruffy, with gingerish hair and a touch of humour to his face. 'It's very beautiful,' I said. 'Like nowhere else. But a little sad.'

'It is very poor,' said the driver.

'And strange, don't you think?' said the other, screwing a finger against his temples. 'For we have a mad leader. A Caligula, no?'

I said that it was impossible not to suspect something of the kind. There was the constant irony of cycling through sleepy villages, like the one we had just come from, where, every fifty yards along the road, there was a sign: CEAUȘESCU EPOCA GLORIOASA; CEAUȘESCU PACE, PROGRES.

'Good,' the scruffy one said. 'It is good you can understand those.'

It threatened to rain and I could not stop for long, but before I went on I asked what they knew about the riots. They were free to talk here, protected by the anonymity of the road. They said they did not know for sure what had taken place before the Party building. The driver had gone there but saw so many militia around that he had turned back. As for what had happened since, he was bitter. '"Yes, yes," they say. "No pay cuts. Go back to work, go home." And they try to buy us with food. But six months after, pay and food are like before. And in six months some people have gone, "moved away" and we do not know where. Even now, people are picked up by the police.'*

Braşov showed not a sign of the disturbances. Peter's guidebook even recommended a restaurant, the Carpathian Stag. I suspended disbelief. But before we could indulge in roast venison and wild boar it would be necessary to change money at the Hotel Carpati. The ground floor was like a deserted departure lounge, an expanse of brown carpet gloomy beneath a chequered ceiling of fluorescent panels lit at random. There was a hard-currency shop, closed, displaying in its window imported coffee, shampoo and peanuts, and a smash-proof glass capsule labelled 'Change', inside which a woman sat between towers of paper. As we approached with our chequebooks she slid open the service window, snapped, '*Dix minutes, attendez dix minutes,*' and slammed it shut again. We sat down. Her fingers counted wads of banknotes and flickered over calculator buttons. Her lips mouthed silent numbers. Now and then she took up one of the half-dozen rubber stamps that were arranged on the desk before her, each with its individual ink pad, and stabbed it at a page. After ten minutes she opened the window again. 'I see you are English. I am sorry, I had thought that you were French. Ten minutes, please.'

After fifteen minutes more she called us over. She tried a smile but it was worn out. She had a tense shadow of prettiness. 'I am sorry. Such a quantity of paper. You can have no idea what such bureaucracy means.' She took Peter's cheque and passport and started to fill out an exchange form. 'For each form here I must make another form, and check the calculations and stamp them afterwards. And I must do all these before I can leave. I live out of town and the last bus goes at eight o'clock. By eight o'clock I will not finish. Please sign here.' But Peter saw she had made a small mistake in the figures. She reeled back when he mentioned it as if he had accused her of a crime. 'No, no, no, that is terrible. Please, you must believe me, I do not mean to make such a mistake. Never before have I done such a thing!' She calmed when he did not press her; she said it was just that there were so many forms to do.

She redid the calculation and started the procedure again, leafing the

* At the time of writing, April 1989, I read news of a young man immolating himself in front of British skiers at the resort of Poiana Braşov. He left behind him no name, just a note pinned to a tree: Stop the murders in Braşov.

carbons between the triplicate sheets. Peter asked if she could not simply correct and have him initial the original form. She answered, with a look of horror, that that was quite unacceptable; 'they' would never believe this; a new form was absolutely required. But when she wrote it out the poor woman was so distracted that she repeated her original mistake. She started to cry. Only on the third attempt were the figures inserted correctly, and she meticulously stamped cancellations on the six ruined sheets and stapled each one individually into her ledger. 'You do not know. How can you know? For you it is different. You come from another world.'

And we had added to her workload for nothing. The Carpathian Stag and most of the other restaurants in the town were reserved for wedding parties; weddings always took place on Sundays and the parties were lavish all-afternoon and all-night affairs for which families might save up money and rations for three years in advance. Only one restaurant could serve us, with the one dish on the menu: a plate of chips and sinewy meat that neither of us had the strength to finish. It brought to mind too closely the tired horses we passed on the roads.

We went out and walked the streets, gawping, like the rest of the uninvited, at the wedding celebrations. Close to the old square was a restaurant that must have been imposing fifty years earlier. It had a huge plate-glass window, now cracked from parapet to pavement and held together with giant studs. The interior glowed with raspberry-coloured wallpaper, and tables with white linen cloths stretched between heavy fluted columns. At one table a row of stolid women sat before a heap of emptied bottles, at another, a row of ageing men; while at the end of the room the young danced and the bride was tossed from hand to hand like a piece of froth.

'You should get yourself invited,' Peter said to me. 'It would give you something cheerful to write about. And you could bring out some food.' But all the plates on those long tables had already been picked clean. There was bread and jam in my hotel room.

Next day I had to turn south finally for Bucharest. Peter was going on to Sibiu. We went to a bar for a parting drink and spent a fretful half-hour or more waiting to be served. A waitress passed by at long intervals with a trolley of bottles or glasses but never stopped beside us. Was this a private bar, or had we failed to note some system, take a ticket or make an order at the door? We looked around and saw that, although the room was smoky and packed as a German beer cellar, only a small minority of men had drinks before them.

The youth sitting opposite leant across and spoke in English. 'For us, the beer is an illusion. I tell you this so that you do not worry. You may wait one hour. You may wait four. It may be in front of you at ten but that is when they close. Or it may not come until tomorrow morning and then it is you who will not be here.'

'So why do you come?'

'This bar has the fastest service in the town.'

15

I spent a cold night in the mountains just beyond Sinaia. It was too late in the year to camp so high. In the morning I went back to the town for a recuperative breakfast at the Hotel Palace, category Lux. Sinaia was once a fashionable resort and the royal summer residence. The sound of a fountain drifted up through parkland trees to the coloured umbrellas on the hotel terrace. At the garden's edge a high fence enclosed a replica of the Monte Carlo casino, white as the hotel amid the green. It was used now for state receptions and guarded by soldiers. Out of sight somewhere high above was the old Royal Palace, though the tourist office told me that it was closed for reconstruction.

Rich American and British voices sounded in the restaurant. Most of them belonged to women, sleek, well-preserved women dressed at the best department stores. I caught sight of myself in a mirrored door and felt a vagabond. Voyages Jules Verne had brought an English-speaking Orient Express tour here for the night, to this élite island where food shortages were unknown. I ate a huge breakfast and talked with their guide. I told him of the picture of pre-war Sinaia in the novels of Olivia Manning; did he know what had happened to the Royal Palace? He said that it had been closed for a long time. It once had very fine gardens but no-one knew what had become of them. (Was it now perhaps a presidential retreat?) He was interested to hear how Olivia Manning described Bucharest at the end of the 1930s. He said it was impossible nowadays to learn much about the history of the city – almost as hard as to guess its future. 'Whatever you have seen of new development in other towns, there is more of it in Bucharest, so much more. We who live there do not know what is happening. Maybe the architects do. I hope so.' I need spend no more than a day there, he advised; or why not take it easy in Sinaia and miss out Bucharest altogether?

Before he swept his tour back into their air-conditioned coach he came to take a look at my bike and compare its merits with those of his own Sputnik. I lightened my pannier by giving him my copy of *The Balkan Trilogy*. I had a chapter still to read but it would mean more to him than it would to me.

Bucharest seemed a Movietone city, like the black-and-white Paris of a post-war newsreel but a Paris that had been blitzed. I came in from the north down a shattered road whose surface switched from tarmac to rutted mud to cobbles criss-crossed with tramlines that trapped cycle wheels. Past the half-formed fringe was high-rise suburb and past that the city proper, pitted with building sites where random bombs might have fallen.

I found a hotel in the centre, a 1920s building whose art-deco streamlining exaggerated the height of its eight floors. A half-dozen other hotels I'd tried were full, and their staff had told me that every room in Bucharest was taken, but here the thin man at the reception desk said that I should wait, that perhaps something would turn up. I sat three hours in a red armchair near the base of the spiral stairwell until a tour of Russian women came down, by chattering relays, in the birdcage lift. The thin man nodded and gave me a single room, with balcony, on the seventh floor.

Three streets came to a junction below. The people who crossed between the few slow cars looked deliberate and drab like a population accustomed to war. They seemed a past generation: briefcase-carrying men in belted macs waiting by the public telephone; women, square-shouldered, straight-skirted, hair under tight control, who met their friends and went to consume ersatz coffee and cakes in the café opposite.

I walked around. The streets had a strange sameness beneath a colourless sky. Buildings of brown stone and brownish concrete, nineteenth-century banks, turn-of-the-century hotels and modern apartment blocks all shared the blank face of neglect. The juxtaposition of styles was crude, as if pieces of innumerable other cities had been shuffled roughly together. Only momentarily did the miniature form of a Byzantine church, with patterned brickwork and a porch carved with arabesques, break through the dreariness. And down by the base of the grand Calea Victoriei I came the first evening to a district – not so much a district as a remnant of one – where the houses had a Balkan lightness and small shops pressed together across streets that were narrow and dense with life.

*   *   *

It is a hollow pretension now to call Bucharest the Paris of the East. Sure, you can still see that the architects of the late nineteenth century, like the rest of new Romania's intellectuals, took their style from the French. Boyar families had florid palaces built on the Calea Victoriei and the fashionable bourgeoisie moved to high-ceilinged apartments behind curving balconies or villas on suburban streets lined with pollarded limes. Boulevards cut through the city and a great avenue swept up from the end of the Calea Victoriei towards the great park on the outskirts. In 1922 this avenue acquired a triumphal arch. But it is a poor imitation of the Champs Elysées, meagre, out of scale. The arch, which had to be re-erected in reinforced concrete in 1935 as the original shoddy structure was falling down, has no Napoleon to celebrate. It commemorates the establishment of Greater Romania, România Mare, following the first war, when Transylvania was at last united with the other states; it is ironic that only a decade after the monument was completed in its present form România Mare lost two great slices of land: the northern Bukovina and Bessarabia to Russia, and the southern Dobrudja to Bulgaria.

At the end of the avenue, way beyond the arch, is the Scînteia building which houses the official Romanian press and its printing works. It is massive, monumental and angular. When it was built, no longer Paris but Moscow was the inspiration.

Radu's family offered a retreat. When we met in Sibiu he had told me to get in touch in Bucharest, and how to find the rambling bungalow where they lived, down a dirt track close to the edge of the city. I spent two long afternoons in the vine shade of their courtyard; down here on the plain it was still warm to sit out when the sun shone.

There were four generations in the house: Radu's grandmother, his parents and his six-year-old son, as well as himself; his wife was estranged. The family had moved out from the centre fifteen or twenty years earlier in search of a garden. The sturdy bungalow they built stood out among the near shanty housing of newcomers, a smug compound behind high metal railings. In front was a bright strip of roses, dahlias and white tobacco plants but the area at the side of the house was taken up with rows of vegetables, hen run and pig sty. Radu's father, also called Radu – as every eldest son in the Maniu family had been called for generations – had been forced to relinquish his flower garden piece by piece during the last six or seven years as the national austerity measures had taken hold. Radu senior was a stooped man with a long sallow face. His eyes were soft and dreamy. When he came home from his engineering office he mournfully tidied his few flowers, plucking off dead heads and aphids, then resigned himself to the odd peasant chore before changing into striped pyjamas to lounge through the evening served by his women.

It was the women who did most things, broke the chickens' necks and plucked them, tended and picked the fruit and vegetables, pickled and bottled them or spread them out to store in the cool of the garage. The two men organised the killing of the pigs, and Radu senior reserved for himself the pleasure of making wine, for which his wife had prepared clean glass jars. Zoraida was a sturdy woman with broad back and hips equal to more than the work she did. The old woman, her mother-in-law, did the lighter jobs, cooking and making the *tzuica*, the light plum brandy which she drank with every meal from breakfast on. Raluca was eighty, slight and sprightly, with the wide brown eyes and mobile face of a marmoset. She talked incessantly, quite unbothered by my minimal Romanian; she managed to communicate an amazing amount in her expressions and gestures, her crisp speech and her old woman's repetitions. Some things I may have got quite wrong but I always felt I had the gist of what she was saying: Romanian words are often guessable.

Her sewing machine was out on a table in the courtyard. She sat at it in faded apron and peasant kerchief and worked on an elaborate garment she was making for herself, of black lace and black lining; it looked like a pre-war cocktail dress.

'Radu said that he met you in Sibiu?' She probed for information. I let out that he had had Doina with him.

She put down her sewing. 'That's what we thought. He would not say but we thought as much. What did you make of Doina?' But she did not let me answer: 'She works in his office, you know, but she's only a typist, not an engineer! That girl doesn't show her face here. Now, his wife, the boy's mother, is a nice woman . . .' And so it went. Zoraida joined us and nodded support at all her mother-in-law said. It was clear that they were determined to stick the marriage together again; the odds were against Doina. Raluca reached out her hand and rubbed the fingers against the thumb: 'She chases Radu for his money. The little gold-digger!'

After all, the Manius were not just anyone. Raluca reminded me that her husband had owned a Rolls Royce. She showed me his photograph, a stern man in high collar and small stiff moustache.

She took up her work again. She was proud of the dress; it would show how slim she still was. If only she could get some really elegant stockings to wear with it, but that was impossible nowadays. A few years ago perhaps, but not now. I said I could send some from England.

'But they must be fine ones. Black, with flowers but the flowers must not be too big. You know the type? Elegant.' She gave me the size and said perhaps I should send two pairs so that she had one as standby.

Taking two pins from between her lips, she talked on. The Manius' wealth was little compared with that of her own people, who had owned an estate in northern Bessarabia, in Russia now. She had long been married and living in the Maniu house on this side of the present Romanian border when the Soviets took Bessarabia in June 1940. Her brother had refused to leave his land and was sent to Siberia, where he stayed on even after he could have returned: what point was there in going back? And what a grand house theirs had been. When it was built her father knew nothing of architecture; he went to the builders and instructed them only to make it the most beautiful in the district. It was, she said, and the biggest. A year or two previously, Radu had gone to Russia and visited it, seen it now, a little crumbling, divided now into three: part was the mayor's residence, part the local cinema and part a workers' club.

I asked if she had pictures but there was nothing. Those of her family who had left ahead of the Soviets had had time to take with them only a few essentials.

Radu's car came to the gate and the little boy ran to open it. We were going into the city for dinner. Raluca asked quickly whether Doina would be there. She gave a complacent grin when I said no; I was no threat, I was only there for a couple of days.

Radu drove me round the city.

'First I will take you to see the airport.' We crossed the suburbs, through acres of prefabricated flats and then a stretch of open land. 'The international airport has one of the longest runways in Eastern Europe. Three thousand five hundred metres. Ceauşescu always builds the biggest.' It was hard to distinguish pride from irony in his voice.

'Is it so busy?' I asked.

'Not today. Today there is no requirement for such a runway. But there is the capacity for forty planes to land each hour. That is second only to Moscow.'

We drove up to the terminal and circled back towards the city down a dual carriageway of flawless asphalt. 'This is our three-lane highway. It begins by the airport and runs to the main city boulevards. Foreign heads of state come down it when they visit Bucharest.'

Close to the airport was the showcase new village of Otopeni. It consisted of a group of small apartment blocks in post-modernist style, concrete with red brick ornament, not unlike the housing many British councils now pride themselves on building. Radu pointed them out. 'Otopeni is the prototype of the new village Ceauşescu wants to build. You can see for yourself that these are not the tower blocks the Hungarians talk about. The houses are not too high, only four or five floors, with nice balconies, well built. Perfectly liveable.'

(An article in *Stern* magazine, October 1988, reported however that behind their innocuous façades the prefabricated houses of Otopeni offered spartan accommodation, that they were patched together, that the stairwells were bare concrete and the doors plywood, and that each family unit offered a mere ten square metres of living space.)

'You can be romantic about the villages,' Radu went on. 'But do you not see that they must be modernised? This is the twentieth century. We are a small country and we have many problems. The population will increase. We need land to feed ourselves. You know how the villages are: they spread along the road, each house with its yard and garden and patch of field. What a waste of land that could be farmed! Then also the houses are old and do not have modern facilities. Villages are dotted all over the country and no proper roads go to them. It would not be practical or economic to renew all those houses and build new roads everywhere.'

Radu seemed to have swallowed whole the orthodox view. ROMANIA: CEAUŞESCU: PROGRES. He did not question the premises to its facile logic. Like many of the middle-class of the third world, he was ashamed of what he saw as his country's backwardness; he equated development with new concrete. Yet he had told me when we met before that he had a dream of one day retiring to a little house by the village of Dragoslavele in the sub-Carpathians: I could not imagine this dream played out with Dragoslavele amalgamated into an 'agro-industrial complex'. Perhaps long habituation to dogma caused him automatically to separate what seemed paper plans and mere words from the reality that touched himself? His position constantly shifted before I could take a sure bearing. And I did not believe this was only caution: he spoke with far more force than caution demanded.

I mentioned something I had heard, that the Party would be glad simply to be relieved of the embarrassment caused by the present situation, by which peasants working in the mountains produced more per acre than collectives on the richer soil of the plain.

'Who told you that?'

'A Pole I met on a camp site.'

'Well, what do you expect?'

I tried new tacks. Wasn't it just a question of mountains and Mohammeds: surely it would be just as costly to demolish existing villages, build new ones and move thousands of people? He did not agree. I asked what he thought it would mean to villagers to be torn from home, tradition and from the piece of land where they kept their poultry and grew their vegetables. Even in the capital city his own family needed their land.

He said they would be given small allotments close to the apartment blocks. 'But yes, I admit that the plan is hard. It is coming too fast. People should be allowed to choose.'

'They might want to stay as they are.'

'No, they would move in the end. They would see that it was necessary. Only the change would be more gradual. But Ceauşescu is a rigid man and he is old. He wants to see his New Romania before he dies.'

We wove through the strip of lakes and parkland that borders the north of the city. Radu paused on a bridge where a narrow inlet of land divided two straggling lakes. 'The lake on the left used to be ours. Now it is his. His house is behind the trees.' I could see nothing beyond the willows on the far bank.

Down one of the main boulevards we passed an ostentatious modern tower: 'The Intercontinental Hotel, built by the Americans; it is the tallest building in the city. Inside you do not know you are in Romania.' Close by was the new National Theatre. 'There were many good designs but he chose this one and added a few ideas of his own. I think it was hard for him to picture the building from the architects' plans so he waited to see it in real life. Then he had the front rebuilt three times. It is our monument to bad taste.'

The road crossed a vast construction site. We parked and walked back up a slight ramp to the roundabout at its centre. The roundabout was already turfed and immaculately planted with bedding; a dry concrete pool held the workings of a fountain. The Boulevard of the Victory of Socialism was huge; a hundred and twenty metres wide,

Radu said. Down the middle ran a stripe of new turf and the shells of Taj-Mahal pools stuck with fountain spouts. This was flanked by avenues of stripling chestnuts beneath ornate and faintly Belle Epoque lamp posts. We walked up between the ten-storey apartment blocks. These were fashionably post-modernist, with a banal clutter of columns, parapets, balconies of iron and concrete, friezes and moulded rosettes, each section variously finished, smooth or rusticated, faced in stone or marble. The flats were nearing completion; shops on the ground floor had already been allotted names: *Cofetarie*, *Elegant*, *Cordial*.

The avenue echoed the totalitarian projects of the 1930s, Mussolini's EUR and Speer's thwarted designs for Berlin. Neo-classicism seems to be obligatory for a régime that remembers Rome. This plan may have lacked the amphitheatric grandeur of its forerunners; there were no triumphal columns, nor yet were there eagles on the Romanian flag. But it was far more impressive simply because its concrete was raw: it expressed a living not a historic power.

'Who will have the flats?'

'Party people.' But Radu looked proud. 'What do you think? It is very modern.'

It was his opinion I wanted to hear. I teased him, said the style was rather bourgeois, nothing like Fritz Lang's *Metropolis*.

'Bourgeois? No, it's peasant.' He spat the word out. 'Like a rich peasant's place.' He seemed to be forgetting his own origins.

'What was here before?'

'Nothing much. It was a very cramped, old district, full of little houses and the slums of Jews.'

Ahead was a colossal building whose form blocked the full breadth of the Boulevard. It loomed up against a violet sky where the sun had just set. Its scale was hard to comprehend until we reached the crescent space immediately before it and I saw the wings that extended on either side and tripled its width. The building stood on an artificially shaped hill of bare earth; the central section was eleven storeys high and unfinished. Radu said that it was to be as deep as it was broad and to run almost as far below ground as above.

'What is it for?'

'It is our president's new palace. This great area where we stand is for rallies of the people. Underground, Ceauşescu will have a nuclear shelter, with a hydraulic escape mechanism to transport him there. Behind the palace will be helicopter pads etcetera and a park greater than all the others in the city.'

There was still a note of admiration in his voice. He said that when Gorbachev came to Bucharest, Ceauşescu brought him here: 'What is this for?' Gorbachev had gasped. 'The United Nations?'

A hum of machinery came from the building even in the evening: work would go on all night. Scores of trucks and bulldozers passed across the crescent. Ten cranes hovered over the flat roof. Four lifts moved up and down the walls. An ant army of workers flooded out through the dense scaffolding of the Corinthian portico and down the side of the bare brown mound. Most of the workers, men and women, wore khaki uniforms and white tin hats. They marched in regular battalions. Radu told me that soldiers and convicts had been brought to work here. 'Ceauşescu is a man in a hurry. Work began only four years ago; see how far it has come. As I told you, he is old and perhaps he is sick. He must have it finished soon.'

We turned to go back. In the east the Boulevard petered out in works that were still scarcely begun. The plan was that it would run three kilometres to a vast new square containing a monument to the Victory of Socialism. It was possible to make out only the nearest buildings and the mantis outlines of cranes through a thick greyish mist. I said I would like to see it on a clear day; this evening was too foggy.

'That is not fog. In Romania we do not have the required meteorological conditions for fog.'

'What is it then? Pollution?'

'No. There is no industry around here, only residential districts. It is construction dust.'

When we got back to the car I felt free to speak as I could not under the shadow of the building. 'Radu, it is mad. I have been travelling in this country, I have seen and you know how poor it is. This project must drain away whatever money Romania has!'

'It costs nothing.' His blue eyes looked coolly back. 'It is only *lei*, not dollars or deutschmarks. The materials and the labour are all Romanian.'

'But materials and labour can be converted into dollars and deutschmarks.'

He chose to be blind to my point. 'You come from the West. You do not understand our economy here.'

The following day he gave me an illustration. I was in his house and he showed me his tape system – which was extravagant even by Western standards – and video. I already suspected that he was involved, to some extent, in black marketeering. Large sums of dollars and even larger ones of *lei* must have been necessary to buy these in the hard currency shops, in the days when it was still possible to buy high quality foreign products. He set a lot of store by the Japanese brand names. 'People say that we Romanians are snobs. Perhaps we are. We are a civilised people, like the French. It is important to us that we have what is good: Hitachi, Toshiba, JVC. You think it is strange how much Romanians will pay for a pack of Kent cigarettes. It is because they are the best. The cost does not matter. You think because you have to change money at the hotels that the *lei* has value. But it is paper. Many of us have money, much money, but it serves no purpose.'

He pulled from a cupboard a plastic bag and emptied it on to the floor. It made a mountain of blue hundred-*lei* notes and savings bonds of larger denominations. 'There is half a million *lei*.* Tell me what I can do with it.'

---

* Approximately £28,000 at the official exchange rate; perhaps a sixth of that at the black-market rate.

16

The Ministry of Truth contained, it was said, three thousand rooms above ground level, and corresponding ramifications below.

George Orwell, *1984*

I went back alone to the Boulevard. It was impossible to work out where I was according to city map or guidebook published in 1980. A compass would have served better since the new district was geometrically arranged. I could identify only a couple of the old monuments described in the book. The Church of the Patriarchate stood on a hill just off the central Piaţa Unirii; the approach road ran off at a lone diagonal in the new grid. The sixteenth-century church of Mihai Vodă had been moved from its original site, which fell awkwardly beneath the planner's ruler, and stood adrift now among apartment blocks instead of monastery buildings.

It has been reported in the West that almost a quarter of the area of old Bucharest was demolished to make way for the new constructions – and the work was by no means finished. By most accounts, the destroyed Uranus-Antim district consisted not of what Radu crudely condemned as 'Jewish slums' but of a confusion of tight, almost oriental streets and stuccoed early nineteenth-century villas. (A pocket of ochre houses remained when I was there, close to the new 'commercial agro-industrial complex' as the market was now called; it was true that these were slummy, overcrowded, tumbledown: but this seemed the result of deliberate neglect.) Sixteen churches dating from the sixteenth, seventeenth and eighteenth centuries disappeared, three monasteries, three synagogues, the remains of two palaces and a fine nineteenth-century hospital. Some of the demolitions took place surreptitiously: the Spirea Veche church was entirely destroyed at night in what was claimed to be a gas explosion. Uncounted tens of thousands of people were evicted from their homes in the course of the demolitions, often at no more than a day's notice.

It was credible that the new blocks would provide more housing, fulfilling one of the stated objectives of the scheme, though unlikely that it would be for the same people. Undeniably the inner-city road system would be simplified; and the new administrative and political centre would offer the most extensive facilities: in the palace there would be room enough even for the files of the *Securitate*, which theoretically included samples of type from every typewriter in the country, according to the legal licence requirement, and other such trivia as reports of citizens' conversations with wandering foreigners like myself.

A single symbolic aim, however, overwhelmed these practicalities. In 1984 when work began Ceauşescu declared, in the habitually ponderous and incoherent style so imitated by his flatterers, the inauguration of 'grandiose and luminous foundations of this epoch of profound transformations and innovations, of monumental buildings which will persist across the ages'. It was to be a monument to himself, or at least to the epoch which bears his name.

This megalomaniac vision had come a long way in four years. Standing before it I suddenly saw Ceauşescu's other plans with a new realism. Systemisation looked attainable. Until then the idea of the destruction of half the country's thirteen thousand villages and the entire restructuring of rural life, had seemed an ambition too huge to contemplate, the more so in view of the chronic shortages and inefficiency that were encountered everywhere. Convincing as the official pronouncements might sound, it was tempting to dismiss them as slogans, a fantasy, a ruse to scare the rural population into greater submission; I felt that the same instinctive escapism led to other people's reticence on the issue, that and perhaps also a superstition that to take the plan too seriously might speed its progress.

The rural resettlement scheme known as *Sistematizarea* was first adopted as part of the Party programme as long ago as 1972 but received exact form only in the spring of 1988. It aims at an instant and stunningly literal application of the measure defined by Marx in *The Communist Manifesto* as 'gradual abolition of the distinction between town and country'; in the current jargon, 'homogenisation'. As Party officials have stated, the end product is to be the 'new man'. Some details have been published: there will be two main types of apartment building, one for peasants, one for workers and intellectuals, each offering a set number of rooms and a small allotment, peasants receiving larger plots than the others. Communal baths will be provided (suggesting that individual bathrooms will not be) and each village will have a civic centre known as the 'Hymn to Romania House of Culture'. No mention has been made of churches. The programme is to be implemented in three phases for completion by the year 2000.

Vocal opposition has come from a brave handful of people. Doina Cornea, a lecturer at Cluj University, wrote in August 1988 an open letter to Ceauşescu which was published in the West; she was put under house arrest soon after. She pointed out that the villages, with their unbroken folk culture, their churches which survived Mongol and Turkish invasions, are the spiritual centre of Romanian life; that to demolish them would be to 'strike at the very soul of the people'. Wholesale systemisation would have a terrifying absoluteness, destroying the culture of an entire nation – as it must if it is to create a 'new man'. It is perhaps because this is so unthinkable that foreign observers initially found it easier to accept the subjective Hungarian interpretation of the plan, as an attack aimed specifically at themselves: there are many more historical precedents for the persecution of ethnic minorities.

The programme has a fanatic ring of Stalinist orthodoxy. Some see in it a plot to bring the villagers as much as the townspeople under the controlling eye of the *Securitate*, making Romania the ultimate police state. There is also a sinister rumour, told me by a Romanian exile in London, that Ceauşescu was intensively trained for ten years by Stalin's KGB. She said there was a mysterious gap in his biography, over the years immediately following the war, where known facts contradicted the official version of his whereabouts; it is suggested that during this period he was effectively brainwashed to carry out the Russian strategy of the day: a plan to so reduce the distinct Romanian culture that it could never threaten the land connection between the Slav nations, Russia and Bulgaria and problematical Yugoslavia. Ceauşescu, a young Party member just out of wartime jail, a semi-educated shoemaker's apprentice, was ideal material for indoctrination: forty years later he would fight on like a lost Japanese soldier in an island jungle. Yet even this sensational story seems a reduction to rational motives, casting the original blame on to an outside enemy. The truth, surely, was madder than that?

I learnt when I got back to England that it was during my stay in Romania that the first village clearances took place, in areas very close to Bucharest. Notice was brief and evictions were swift. Four villages were amalgamated on the site of the largest, in unfinished blocks on streets that were still unpaved. The sewerage system was not completed, water and electricity had not been connected, and no stables or hen coops existed to which people could move their livestock. Amid the emotion of departure from old family homes people found that they must begin the demolition themselves, taking with them any salvageable wood – beams, doors and window frames – for use as firewood. Within a month the old sites had been thoroughly bulldozed and cleared of rubble, and road signs naming the extinct villages had been removed.

The national history museum was in the Calea Victoriei. There were few visitors in its dim nineteenth-century halls and barrel-vaulted corridors. There was a school group on the ground floor, brought for instruction on the Trajan's Column friezes, and in a basement gallery walled in purple felt a foreign delegation politely admired Romanian gold, the beaten gold ornaments of the Dacians and medieval jewelled monstrances and crowns. On the first floor the attendant was reluctant to turn on the lights: 'No, go on up to the top floor. The *Omagiu*. Up and left at the top.'

Omagiu: homage. To Ceauşescu, who else? In room after room, arranged by province and labelled with the names of collectives, factories and Young Pioneer groups, was an extraordinary array of objects presented by the nation. They ranged from the predictable commemorative plaques and trophies, samples of regional embroideries and craftwork, to one-off manufactured pieces. A carpet factory had made a rug in which Ceauşescu's head rose god-like from the clouds above a sea of tiny figures; another, one in which he stood before the massed smoke stacks of a gigantic industrial plant. A glassworks had had his image engraved on a ruby red vase. Rival porcelain makers had produced huge and lurid jars on which his portrait was framed by golden scrolls, entwined flowers and doves, even emerging from a pink-tinged vista of high-rise blocks. One machine factory had given a golden model tractor, another a golden bulldozer.

A tapestry in a gold frame, so finely worked that it is only when you come close that you can distinguish the stitches. Ceauşescu smiles his tenor's smile, arms overflowing with pink roses as after a rapturous curtain call. An oil painting: in a white safari suit like an ageing film star on the Riviera, he raises a plump right hand to acknowledge the cheers of clamouring masses. The portraits give him a cheap glamour. Though a statesmanlike greyness streaks his hair he is allowed to age little beyond a distinguished fifty. Only exceptionally does a dark suit and workers' cap or tin hat suggest an air of seriousness, as he towers over a new shipyard or presses a button to open the gates of a dam. The image is lightweight; there is no appearance of the steel or charisma of a Stalin or Mao.

By his side, Elena is depicted as the youthful mother of the nation. There is no grey in her hair, for her image is frozen a decade or so earlier than her husband's. Blonde freshness is considered appropriate for a 'Heroine of the Socialist Republic of Romania' – no matter that she was to receive the title only on her seventieth birthday. She too is offered pink roses, by a boy whose face glows in the golden light that radiates from behind her head: the picture recalls representations of the Virgin Mary; its religiosity is disturbing. Only one portrait gives a more truthful representation, of an elderly woman with careworn face, hair severely drawn back, hard blue eyes; and this depicts the scientist Ceauşescu, a white-coated Marie Curie.

When Ceauşescu came to power in 1965 he seemed a harmless figure. He came from the dimness of the Party administration and few people even knew who he was. His policies developed from those of his predecessor, Gheorghiu-Dej, and he presided over an optimistic period of liberalisation in the late 'sixties. Simmering Romanian nationalism was cheered by his stance of independence from Moscow, most dramatically demonstrated in August 1968 when he refused to send Romanian troops alongside the other Warsaw Pact armies into Czechoslovakia. The pose went down even better in the West, where he was hailed as an open-minded maverick and favoured as a potential friend in the Cold War. This wishful image persisted though his opposition to Russia went only skin-deep, though the personality cult and the corresponding oppression at home expanded, and though his ambitions revealed themselves as thoroughly Stalinist. From the start he planned massive industrial and construction projects such as the development of monster metallurgical plants and grandiose, if ecologically lethal, schemes for irrigation and for drainage of the Danube Delta. In 1973 he even announced an intention to complete the notorious Danube–Black Sea Canal, on which perhaps thousands of forced labourers had died before work had been halted twenty years earlier.

During the 'seventies foreign tours took Ceauşescu all over the world, including London, where he stayed at Buckingham Palace, and Washington to see President Carter. He earned a name for peace largely due to his refusal to join with the rest of the Warsaw Pact countries in breaking ties with Israel after the 1967 war, and subsequent involvement in the peace process. (Doves have fluttered around his image ever since: most grotesquely in the entrance hall of the history museum where three stuffed ones peck like vultures at the carcase of a broken and disembowelled plaster missile.) And it was not only his vanity that prospered: Romania was awarded the coveted privilege of most-favoured-nation trading status with the United States. This was renewed yearly until as recently as 1987, despite protests. Only since the transformation of superpower politics brought about by Gorbachev has it suited America to withdraw its favours, and Western European governments to put pressure on Romania over human rights.

The final room in the *Omagiu* testifies to Ceauşescu's diplomatic triumphs. The glass cases are crammed with foreign awards: broad-ribboned medals from innumerable African and South American republics, from fellow Socialist states and not a few from the West. Ceauşescu has the British Knight Grand Cross of the Order of the Bath and the French *Légion d'Honneur*, besides honorary citizenships of Texas and Disneyland. And although her own chemistry qualifications are obscure, the Academician Comrade has honorary degrees and fellowships from universities as far afield as Islamabad and Liberia – as many caps and gowns as Imelda Marcos had shoes.

Outside it was fine, though it had rained in the morning. Umbrellas were furled but men still wore their dark hats and wartime raincoats. Beneath the tarnished gilt mirrors in Capşa's once-famous restaurant a middle-aged woman with red lipstick and red nails laid her cotton gloves and sunglasses on the tablecloth and laughed too loudly. She seemed a vulgar shadow of the period élite. On the streets I noticed a man in spats who held a cane in his hand; a couple of other men wore the double-breasted suits of 'thirties cads, hair oiled and a touch long, hats with overlarge brims. Their exhibitionism only defined the anonymity of the crowd.

Further up the Calea Victoriei was the sombre square before the former Royal Palace. Pedestrians were thinly scattered over the cobbled expanse. As I started to walk across, a policeman blew his whistle and gestured to me to move away. I noticed that no-one at all stepped into that particular area, which seemed to be reserved for the pigeons. I realised later that the building behind housed the offices of the Party Central Committee.

The despotism of the *Omagiu* had been farcical but at the same time terrifying. Looking at the passing faces I thought not of the people but of what lay behind them. Not that there were any strings to be seen. I felt only how they were ground down into greyness by the everyday humiliations, the interminable queues and the petty restrictions, the nebulous fears and suspicions. And demoralisation made a man manipulable. What difference did it make whether one in three was a *Securitate* informer or whether people merely believed it? The idea was insidious enough. And if the system was that they must talk, must report at least something of their conversations with me, for example, how demoralising those tiny betrayals must be. Rumours of persecutions, beatings, disappearances, lay in shadow far beyond, their reality impossible to determine. All that I could establish was that I saw apathy everywhere. I guessed that this was both the result of oppression and a last protection against it, a last shell of numbness.

I walked down to the Cişmigiu Gardens. These were lovely, intimate gardens. Paths wound round the boating lake to untrodden lawns, to straight avenues of pollarded limes and to creeper-covered tunnels. People sat on the green slatted chairs along the paths and watched the strollers, men clustered around backgammon and chess tables, and lovers necked in shady corners. The formal flowerbeds were hot with colour. Yet I could not find an escape there. As soon as I sat down by the lake a man sat himself beside me, and when I tried again somewhere else another man appeared mumbling words I did not want to understand. Perhaps the Cişmigiu was a well-known pick-up place but I felt then that I had drawn the trouble to me. It was like a superstition: that others could sense in me a sudden vulnerability. Since coming to the city I had lost detachment – the self-possession that surrounds the traveller who always passes on from places and encounters. There are rare moments in travelling when that barrier is broken. Often these are the moments you travel for: the sudden overwhelming impressions, the quick sympathies. But it is often a kind of relief to spring back into cool foreignness, from which you can observe life at a distance as from a boat drifting along a shore. Out there you are a world to yourself, inviolable. Now the boat had come aground.

I made my steps more deliberate. I came to a pergola shrouded in old wisteria; its greyish woody branches snaked around the cast-iron frame. Inside a policeman stood, notebook in hand, before a group of silent young men who looked like students. None of them moved at all as he rapped out questions. I turned away past autumnal heaps of golden rod which had lost its lustre and fell wildly on to purple asters; it reminded me of home.

Close to the exit was a circular bed packed with a pattern of scarlet flowers and silver foliage. As I reached it I felt that another man was following me, saw him from the corner of my eye as he rounded the circle behind me. His steps changed pace as I changed mine. Then quickened to catch up. I turned suddenly for the gate and he stopped. I went back to the hotel; the incident bothered me out of all proportion.

There was a moth on the wall in my room. I remembered a conversation in Oradea. On the white wall in Nicolae's flat was a beautiful moth; the chalky markings on its wings were like aboriginal war paint. I saw it the first night and it was there again on the second. Someone else had noticed too but I could not remember who it was, perhaps Nicolae himself.

'That moth must be happy.' The idea had a theatricality that struck me as very Romanian.

'Why?'

'It's been here two nights when it could have flown away. The window was open.'

I thought: tomorrow morning I shall leave.

I woke to find the city under a dense and chilly fog. It seemed a fog like an English fog, whatever Radu chose to call it.

I wheeled the bike a last time past the unplumbed fountains of the Piaţa Unirii – cycling was not permitted on boulevards. The new palace loomed ahead, bone-white in the greyness.

It was sixty kilometres to the Danube and the border. The road cut through an invisible plain. The mud in the ruts at the edge spattered my legs and a cold froth of moisture gathered on my clothes as I rode into the fog. The sun broke through only around midday when I arrived at the customs post at Giurgiu. Then it grew warm on my back as I sat there on a concrete slab for almost three hours and waited for them to let me go.

One man told me to lay out the contents of my bags; another came and searched through them. He showed interest only in what was written, not in my camera or films. When at last he found my notebook, all the time in another bag on my shoulder, he looked almost satisfied. 'Your impressions?'

'Yes. I write down things I like to remember.'

He pretended to read. 'Ah. Bucharest is beautiful.' And took the book away.

I was ushered to a little cell for a brisk body search. Then, apparently forgotten, I wandered back into the sun. Time enough passed to photocopy my notes more than once. I hoped I had made them illegible, hoped that there was nothing in them that could damage anyone. I wondered if the police knew something: I had talked once of writing, and once I had left a couple of scribbled pages behind in a hotel room – and that in a Category A hotel where they would be well prepared for foreigners. George Smiley would not have approved.

A man I had not seen before handed me my passport and said goodbye. I stayed and asked for my book. Ten minutes later the man who had searched my bags brought it out from the office. 'Your impressions. Very nice.' He smiled like an old friend as he handed it over and patted me on the back.

I rode off. There was nobody else going my way though a long queue of trucks was waiting to enter the country. It was still some distance to the river and the bridge to Bulgaria, which was itself two kilometres long. I could not resist stopping halfway to look at the book, if only to check that the words were still there. I feared I would lose it again when a sentry stopped me at the base of the bridge, laboriously went over my papers again and made a telephone call before letting me pass.

Beneath the iron bridge spread the Danube. The river seemed to slumber still. In pewter streams it slipped around islands of willow and poplar. Their shores were of pale sand. In the navigable channel beyond the last island a chain of black barges passed slowly downstream.

In the Manius' courtyard in Bucharest, Radu's son had played at building a boat. Someone had nailed together for him a rough raft of pieces of plank and firewood, and the boy tied to the mast a sail made from the red triangle of a Young Pioneer's headscarf, so faded that I guessed it must have belonged to his father when he was at school.

'What is it?' I asked.

'*Vapor.*' A liner. He loaded a cargo of green walnuts from the overhanging tree.

I asked where he would go with it. He said he would take the whole family down the Danube to the Black Sea and across it to Australia.

17

It took me less than ten days to get from the Danube to Istanbul.

Bulgaria seemed at first a liberation. Beyond the cranes of the docks and the towers of the workers' flats, the town of Ruse was a frothy piece of Austria washed up far downstream. Its cream-cake town houses and art-nouveau villas turned their backs on the river, away from the sulphurous stain of Romania on the horizon, the pollution that rose from Giurgiu on the opposite bank. In the sunshine the streets were packed, the crowds bright and loud, freed of the sameness that dulled faces over there. Tall women and hefty men in beach-coloured shirts sauntered down the pavements in trainers. Some stopped by a restaurant window to catch a glimpse of the television, check on progress at the Olympic Games in Seoul. In the smoky interior a group of men debated the boxing. I went in and drank a cold beer. It was 1988 again and the world once more seemed a rational place.

Only the Riga Hotel had a Danube view, an aggressive concrete pile of Socialist prestige design. In the restaurant on the mezzanine floor there was dancing on Saturday night. The clientèle had the flash look of Western executives out with women who weren't their wives; they watched the snaky moves of the girl singer, sheathed in black leather and plastically sexy under dim orange lighting. I shared a table with two construction workers, Vasil and Dimiter, who smoked West German cigarettes and drank Johnnie Walker Black Label. They asked the price of whisky and beer in England, the cost of a house, the cost of a video. It sounded expensive to them. After all, wages might not be high in Bulgaria but life was easy; under Socialism nobody had to sweat for their money. And if you needed a bit more cash you could work a stint in Angola. There the pay was good and you saved fast because there was nothing to buy.

Vasil had a brother who lived in Phoenix, Arizona. Fourteen years earlier on a tour to Istanbul he had walked into the American Embassy and asked for asylum. It sounded as if he had done all right in Phoenix. I wondered if Saturday night there was so very different from Saturday night in Ruse.

Vasil said that after his brother had left he had been taken in by the police for questioning. Not once but a few times. The same had happened to most of the family. Was that bad? I asked. No, he said, it was routine; they had been ready for it. I remembered then that the freedom here was only relative after all.

Bulgaria was reputed to be orthodox Communist, hard-line even, but economically successful, and so it appeared on the surface. The clichés of Communism were evident everywhere: red stars, hammers and sickles, billboard exhortations and raw new monuments glorifying independence, Socialism and the historic Bulgar empire. In Ruse on Sunday newlyweds posed for photographs before the war memorial. In front of the memorial in another town schoolgirls did sentry duty, stepping out, stamping and turning in white ankle socks. When I saw that I wanted to look no further, left the town.

I skimmed the landscape. I camped late, rose early. I wanted only to be on the move. On the fourth day I crossed the Balkans by the Shipka Pass. There was a monument at the summit, a thousand steps rising to a tower that commemorated the defence of the pass in the Russo-Turkish War and Bulgaria's subsequent liberation from Ottoman rule. It was a national tourist attraction, drawing to it stout and patriotic coachloads of peasants and workers who panted up, counting the steps as they climbed. A terrace halfway allowed a pause to catch breath and pose for a photograph before a frieze of allegorical lions breaking their chains, then at the top there were postcards to buy and further pictures to be taken before the return to the coach and the drive on to the next monument. On a peak to the east was a colossal abstract sculpture celebrating Communism and Socialism, arrogant on the horizon as the obelisk of a mill-owner on a Lancashire moor.

Beyond the Balkans the road crossed a dusty plain. Endless fields of plough were laid bare beneath a harsh blue autumn sky. Only occasionally a crop of ungathered cotton glimmered white amid the overwhelming brown. The villages had no face to present to the road, shapeless sprawls of low houses of poor red brick or breeze blocks still unplastered. In one I stopped, went into the prefabricated building that was both shop and bar, sat at the formica table to drink an orangeade. At the counter a lackadaisical girl was stacking bags of boiled sweets. The curtain of pink plastic strips across the open doorway slapped in the breeze; beyond lay the road, a few shacks and barns and the dry expanse. On the white wall of one shed was a mural of a cosmonaut walking in space.

The last morning I joined the main highway that ran through the country from Yugoslavia to Turkey and the Middle East. Police stopped me three times at roadblocks on the way to the border.

Then I entered Turkey and came to the town of Edirne. It showed itself suddenly as I rounded a bend: a hillside bubbling with domes and speared by white minarets. The road ran straight into the heart of the town. Here there was no preliminary concrete labyrinth, only a fine bridge over the thin shallow river, a mosque and a Moslem tomb by the verge. Further on, houses piled together in disorder: homes, hotels, shops, offices; wood against stucco against concrete and brick; the balconies tilting and cramped, the spaces between them packed with signs and advertisements. On the pavements beneath, there was anarchy. Shoeshine men squatted before kits of polished brass; above them stood the sellers of watermelon seeds with their glass-sided boxes, weighing the seeds into paper cones that were folded out of pages from children's schoolbooks. A crowd swirled and broke around them. On roadside stalls were mounds and pyramids of fruit: golden quinces, peaches and pears with a pink blush on their sides, purple figs, the ones at the top cut open to reveal crimson, seed-filled hearts. A current swept me into the bazaar, down a honeycomb tunnel that glittered with strings of electric light-bulbs. I went on and came to a restaurant. Spiced lamb, coriander, oily aubergines, yoghurt and honeyed cakes: each flavour seemed new and amazing.

In the shops I bought simple things – a replacement watchstrap, some washing powder – that I had put off buying for days. Even shopping, I remembered, could be fun. It need not be the daily humiliation of shuffling queues, aching legs and wasted time. For an instant, capitalism had made the world like a toyshop before Christmas. You may doubt the principle of the thing, like those who lament that modern Christmas is no more than a materialist feast, but the toys line the shelves in their gaudy shrink-wrapped packages and eyes light up to see them.

Turkey was capitalist, individualist. Inequality was blatant. The young soldiers who stood sentry before the Nato military installation to the west of the town fingered their guns and stared as I walked past, a hard male menace on their unshaven faces. But it was a world that I knew, where I could take a deep breath and stretch. And I relished its orientalness as an escape from the Europe that lay like a weight behind me. Edirne was once the Byzantine town of Adrianople, then the Ottomans made it their capital in the years before the fall of Constantinople. Today it is still Ottoman in character. Clean Islamic forms stand out across the town, mosques, bazaars and caravanserais of pale stone the colour of honey, banded with red sandstone. I went to the great mosque of the Selimiye, where the shadows fell long across the arcaded courtyard and men squatted to wash at a white marble fountain. I walked on to the smaller mosque that topped a hill to the north. The tiles on its walls were the halcyon blue of the Levant. Outside, three ragged boys were flying kites. The small diamonds of red and indigo wheeled high above the turbanned tombstones of the graveyard.

The wind was stronger the next morning when I left Edirne for Istanbul. I felt its full force only when I turned off the main truck route to follow minor roads across the higher land to the north. Up there I had to fight against the gusts for every kilometre. The fields were bare after harvest. All that was left of the sunflower crop was a multitude of broken stalks and an occasional whirl of dry leaves and seedheads. Telegraph poles marked the straight line of the road for miles ahead, running up and down the grain of the land. A local truck stopped and the driver offered a lift. I rode with him for a grateful thirty kilometres, took another lift later that day when the wind had given way to pelting rain. I spent the night in a dismal town whose name I never thought to ask, got up at six the next morning and rode hard for the last long haul. All day it rained. Sometimes close to the road a few houses were gathered by a mosque or behind a stark windbreak of poplars. Any view there might have been of the hills beyond was hidden by pressing cloud.

I came to Istanbul just before dark. It was hard to say quite where the city began. A village swelled into a town, down streets that were churned up by heavy vehicles and lined with mechanics' workshops. Imperceptibly suburb took over and a street plan started to evolve. I guessed at my direction, bewildered in the sudden traffic.

When at last I passed through a gate in the old Byzantine walls I knew I should have felt a kind of elation. For three months this had been my destination. Yet I went blearily through the streets to the Golden Horn. On a bridge I stopped to look at the Asian city across the Bosphorus. Its lights meant nothing to me. I was like a passenger on a train who has slept through his destination, gets off a couple of stops later, stumbling on to the platform with his bags just a second before the whistle. The first thought is not for the place he's come to but for the next train back from the opposite platform.

It was Europe I had set out to see, not just the end of Europe. My true destination must have been lost somewhere, evaded, unrecognised until it was passed. Perhaps it was in the Carpathians, where Slav and German met Latin, Gothic met Byzantine, where Europe's past met Europe's present – or at least one of its most twentieth-century manifestations. Yet what a relief it was that I had not stopped there and had been carried on to the stations beyond.

Less than a year later I see on television a snatch of documentary film smuggled out of Romania. A shot of Sighişoara. The tall arm of a crane cuts across the medieval view. Scaffolding and boards fill a gap that has been torn in the side of the old town beneath the fortified citadel. I knew when I was there that some pied piper was spiriting the people away; I could not imagine that the buildings too could go so fast. I had thought that I was travelling into history. I had forgotten that history itself moves on.

IRINA RATUSHINSKAYA
IN THE BEGINNING

The autobiography of a dissident poet

'This account mordantly sums up the lies that were endemic in pre-Gorbachev Russia. It is also a moving account of how not everyone can be fooled'
D. M. Thomas in the Sunday Telegraph

'The poignancy of Irina's account of her childhood and school-days lies in the fact that there would be nothing extraordinary in the experiences she recalls were they not taking place in a totalitarian state . . . humour is rarely absent . . . tension is maintained throughout'
Virginia Rounding in The Times Literary Supplement

GEORGE PACKER
THE VILLAGE OF WAITING

'Excellent . . . it's about a painful and overwhelming experi-ence of coming of age in a strange country. It strikes one immediately as both truthful and perceptive'
James Fenton

'In 1982–1983 George Packer worked for the Peace Corps as an English teacher in the village of Lavie in Togo, West Africa, and here recounts his occasionally comic, more often poignant, and frequently tragic experiences in sharp, descriptive prose . . . he is at his best when he writes about people, revealing their histories and psychologies with great sympathy and care'
Publishers Weekly

sceptre

LESLEY DOWNER
ON THE NARROW ROAD
TO THE DEEP NORTH

Journey into a Lost Japan

'She is the perfect guide – expert, intrepid, following a dream'
John Carey in The Sunday Times

'One of the principal charms of ON THE NARROW ROAD TO THE DEEP NORTH is that it deals with aspects of Japan which are quite outside any of our stereotyped assumptions . . . Downer has an instinctive insight into the way the Japanese think – a rare commodity which she uses with a marvellous delicacy of touch'
Katie Hickman in The Literary Review

CHRISTINA DODWELL
TRAVELS WITH PEGASUS

A microlight journey across West Africa

'Christina Dodwell is one of those intrepid British female explorers in the great tradition that stretches from Mary Kingsley to Freya Stark'
Daily Express

'Will be as fascinating to the general non-fiction reader as to the converted travel book addict . . . the combination of problems in the air and adventure on the ground makes this one of the best travel books of the last twelve months'
The Oxford Times

sceptre